Motivation and the Moral Sense in
Francis Hutcheson's Ethical Theory

ARCHIVES INTERNATIONALES D'HISTOIRE DES IDEES
INTERNATIONAL ARCHIVES OF THE HISTORY OF IDEAS

46

HENNING JENSEN

Motivation and the Moral Sense in Francis Hutcheson's Ethical Theory

Motivation and the Moral Sense in Francis Hutcheson's Ethical Theory

by

HENNING JENSEN

MARTINUS NIJHOFF / THE HAGUE / 1971

ISBN 90 247 1187 8

PRINTED IN THE NETHERLANDS

To Audrey and Stephen

TABLE OF CONTENTS

PREFACE   IX

INTRODUCTION   1

    Hutcheson's Life and Works   1
    Method of Treatment   6

I. HUTCHESON'S THEORY OF MOTIVATION   8
    The Origins and Distinctive Characteristics of Hutcheson's
    Theory of Motivation   8
    Hutcheson's Refutation of Egoism   13
    Hutcheson's Treatment of Desire and Pleasure   20
    The Calm Desires   23
    The Place of Reason in Conduct   25
    Concluding Comments on Hutcheson's Theory of Moti-
    vation   32

II. HUTCHESON'S MORAL SENSE THEORY   35
    Shaftesbury's Influence   35
    The Epistemological Background of Hutcheson's Moral
    Sense Theory   39
    The Nature and Function of the Moral Sense   42
    The Nature of Moral Judgments   49

III. THE MORAL SENSE AND MOTIVATION   66
    Introductory Statement of Problem   66
    Hutcheson's Criticisms of the Rationalists   68
    The Moral Sense and Motivation   80
    Obligation and motivation   89

Concluding Remarks   102

IV.   MOTIVATION AND THE MORAL SENSE IN HUTCHESON'S LATER
      WORKS   106

 V.   CONCLUDING REMARKS   110
      The Moral Sense and Moral Feelings   110
      The Justification of Moral Judgments   111
      The Nature of Moral Judgments   113
      Motivation and the Moral Sense   118

SELECTED BIBLIOGRAPHY   122

INDEX   126

PREFACE

Although the works of Francis Hutcheson are unfamiliar to most students of philosophy, it cannot be said that he has been entirely ignored. To be sure, most of the recent writers who deal with Hutcheson's philosophy do so in the course of writing about Hutcheson's famous contemporary, David Hume. This is true, for example, of Norman Kemp Smith, whose book entitled *The Philosophy of David Hume* [1] includes much detailed information concerning Hume's indebtedness to Hutcheson. But others have written about Hutcheson on his own account. William R. Scott's *Francis Hutcheson*,[2] although mainly biographical and historical, is well worth reading. In his article "Some Reflections on Moral-Sense Theories in Ethics," [3] C. D. Broad presents a sustained analysis of the sort of theory held by Hutcheson. D. Daiches Raphael's *The Moral Sense* [4] is competent, interesting, and especially valuable in its treatment of epistemological issues surrounding the moral sense theory. William K. Frankena's article entitled "Hutcheson's Moral Sense Theory" [5] is searching and profound. And, most recent of all, a book by William T. Blackstone has appeared entitled *Francis Hutcheson and Contemporary Ethical Theory*.[6]

One of the difficulties encountered in presenting a study of Hutcheson is that all of his books are extremely rare. Fortunately, L. A. Selby-Bigge's

[1] Norman Kemp Smith, *The Philosophy of David Hume* (London: Macmillan and Co., Limited, 1949).
[2] William Robert Scott, *Francis Hutcheson* (Cambridge, Eng.: Cambridge University Press, 1900).
[3] C. D. Broad, "Some Reflections on Moral-Sense Theories in Ethics," reprinted in *Readings in Ethical Theory*, ed. by Herbert Feigl and John Hospers (New York: Appleton-Century-Crofts, Inc., 1952).
[4] D. Daiches Raphael, *The Moral Sense* (London: Oxford University Press, 1947).
[5] William K. Frankena, "Hutcheson's Moral Sense Theory," *Journal of the History of Ideas*, XVI, No. 3 (1955).
[6] William T. Blackstone, *Francis Hutcheson and Contemporary Ethical Theory* (Athens: University of Georgia Press, 1965).

British Moralists,[7] which is again in print, contains Hutcheson's *Inquiry Concerning Moral Good and Evil* and also brief but important selections from Hutcheson's *Essay on the Nature and Conduct of the Passions and Affections, with Illustrations upon the Moral Sense* and from his *System of Moral Philosophy.*

The main purpose of this book is to present an examination of certain problems which arise in Hutcheson's ethical theory with respect to the relationship between his theory of motivation and his moral sense doctrine. These problems come to a head with the question how, according to his theory, moral judgments are practical.

But, it may be exclaimed, surely the study I propose is in familiar territory, well-traversed and unlikely to unfold new vistas! My convictions are quite the contrary. It is true that nothing concerning Hutcheson is as well-documented as his claim that morality is dynamic and that moral judgments must be capable of influencing us to action. Yet it appears to me that few important doctrines have been so ill-documented as regards a truly careful study of exactly how, on his theory, moral judgments are practical and dynamic. In attempting to supply such a study my main interest will not be historical. Although I shall be concerned to note the extent of Hutcheson's influence upon the history of ethics, the problems with which I shall deal are problems which may be related with profit to contemporary discussions of ethical theory.

Apart from my great indebtedness to all of my teachers at Harvard University, I am indebted in particular to Professor Henry D. Aiken for his direction of my initial studies of Hutcheson and to Professors Roderick Firth and Roderick M. Chisholm for their comments and suggestions. Also, I have been helped by a number of criticisms and suggestions made by Professor A. D. Woozley who read most of this book in typescript. Finally, I wish to express my gratitude to my colleagues Professors Ronald D. Milo and Jeffrie G. Murphy for their advice, encouragement, and criticism. The shortcomings and errors which remain are, I insist, my sole responsibility.

---

[7] L. A. Selby-Bigge, ed., *British Moralists* (2 vols., Indianapolis: Bobbs-Merrill Company, Inc., 1964).

INTRODUCTION

HUTCHESON'S LIFE AND WORKS

The history of philosophy includes the names of many persons, famous in their time, whose contributions to human thought have become, if not entirely forgotten, at least surrounded with obscurity. Such a philosopher is Francis Hutcheson. An outstanding writer and teacher, he was unquestionably one of the most influential philosophers of his day. Yet Hutcheson's works are no longer widely read. During the centuries between Hutcheson and ourselves, he has been overshadowed by men such as Butler and Hume. Nevertheless careful study of the history of ethics provides convincing evidence of the importance of Hutcheson's contribution. Since my book will treat this evidence in some detail, I shall present only a few preliminary comments with respect to Hutcheson's importance.

One of the most striking features of Hutcheson's ethical theory is the fact that it is related to some new directions in philosophy which aroused the attention of David Hume. In the introduction to his *Treatise*,[1] Hume refers to Locke, Shaftesbury, Mandeville, Hutcheson and Butler as men who had preceded him in a new approach to the science of man. This new approach, in Hutcheson's case, might be described as the application of empirical methods to the field of ethics. To appreciate this new development it is necessary to remember that those seventeenth century philosophers who had questioned the claims of rationalism in metaphysics and epistemology had not extended their empirical methods to the areas of ethics and social philosophy. Thus we find that Locke, for all of his empiricism, appeals to intuitive moral truths somewhat after the manner of rationalists like Clarke and Cudworth.

There is no doubt, however, that the importance of Hutcheson's

---

[1] David Hume, *A Treatise of Human Nature*, ed. by L. A. Selby-Bigge (Oxford: The Clarendon Press, 1958), p. xxi.

position lies mainly in his defense of the view that moral distinctions are derived from a moral sense. It is true both that his moral sense theory owes much to Shaftesbury and that it serves to prepare the way for the ethical theory of David Hume. Yet Hutcheson's position differs in subtle but important ways from each of these writers and deserves consideration on its own merits. In the course of defending his moral theory he presents refutations of egoism and rationalism which are not only of historical significance, but of lasting interest.

Apart from these larger features of Hutcheson's philosophy, his works are full of provocative ideas ranging from reflections on laughter to observations on slavery.[2] There is also some novelty in Hutcheson's early suggestions concerning a hedonic calculus and in his use of the phrase "the greatest happiness of the greatest number."

Since the most general facts about Hutcheson are not well known, a brief survey of his life and works may help to clarify the background for later chapters.

Francis Hutcheson was born in Drumalig, Ulster, on August 8th, 1694. Both his father, John Hutcheson, and his grandfather, Alexander Hutcheson, were Presbyterian clergymen. His grandfather had come to Ireland from Scotland. After attending a classical school Hutcheson was sent to an "Academy," a small denominational college where he received training in the scholastic philosophy popular at that time. In 1710, when he was 16, he entered the University of Glasgow and remained there for the next six years. During the first four years of this period he studied philosophy, Latin and Greek, and literature in general. The last two years were spent studying theology in preparation for a career in the ministry.

In about 1717, shortly after leaving the University, Hutcheson wrote a letter to Dr. Samuel Clarke, one of England's leading theologians, in which he expressed objections to Clarke's a priori demonstrations of the existence and nature of God. We find here early evidence of the hostility towards rationalistic metaphysics which characterizes Hutcheson's philosophy. Neither Hutcheson's letter nor Clarke's reply, if indeed he wrote one, have been preserved.

After leaving the University Hutcheson returned to Ireland. In 1719 he was licensed to preach and soon received a "call" to a small country church. But at this time some Presbyterian clergymen asked him to open

---

[2] In an article entitled "Hutcheson and the 'Classical' Theory of Slavery" (*Journal of Negro History*, **XXIV**, No. 3 [1939], 263-280), Wylie Sypher maintains that Hutcheson was the first English writer to present an attack on the so-called "classical" theory of slavery.

a private academy in Dublin. Hutcheson agreed and it appears that the academy was a success. He soon became well known in literary and ecclesiastical circles. At some time during the early years of his residence in Dublin he married.

Hutcheson's best known works are the four essays which were written during his residence in Dublin. These were the *Inquiry Concerning Beauty, Order, Harmony, Design* and the *Inquiry Concerning Moral Good and Evil*, published in 1725, and the *Essay on the Nature and Conduct of the Passions* and the *Illustrations upon the Moral Sense*, published together in 1728. The original title given to the first two essays is worth quoting since it provides its own summary of the author's intentions. It was called *An Inquiry into the Original of our Ideas of Beauty and Virtue in two Treatises, in which the Principles of the late Earl of Shaftesbury are explained and defended against the Fable of the Bees; and the Ideas of Moral Good and Evil are established, according to the Sentiments of the Ancient Moralists, with an attempt to introduce a Mathematical Calculation on subjects of Morality.*

In tracing Hutcheson's relations to his contemporaries it is worthwhile keeping in mind the above dates of the publication of Hutcheson's essays as compared with the dates of publication of some of the other famous works published during this intensely active period. Joseph Butler's *Fifteen Sermons* were published in 1726 and his *Analogy of Religion* appeared in 1736. Hume's *Treatise of Human Nature* was published in 1739-40. William Wollaston's *The Religion of Nature Delineated* was privately printed in 1722 and Ralph Cudworth's *Treatise Concerning Eternal and Immutable Morality* was first published in 1731, long after Cudworth's death, which occurred in 1688.

During this period Hutcheson also contributed six letters to the *Dublin Journal*. The first three, which appeared in 1725, were the *Reflections upon Laughter,* directed against the analysis of laughter presented by a follower of Hobbes. The three others, which were printed in 1726, were the *Remarks on the Fable of the Bees*. These six letters were also bound in a collection entitled *Hibernicus's Letters*.

Hutcheson's works soon became the subject of much discussion. Among the more interesting of the criticisms of Hutcheson is the series of letters in the *London Journal* of 1728 written by Gilbert Burnet, who signed his letters "Philaretus," together with Hutcheson's replies. A collection of these letters was published in 1735. In the preface to the *Essay on the Nature and Conduct of the Passions with Illustrations upon the Moral Sense* Hutcheson states that the letters by "Philaretus" gave the first occasion to his fourth essay, the *Illustrations upon the Moral Sense.*

Hutcheson's growing reputation led to his being elected, in 1729, to the chair of moral philosophy at the University of Glasgow. The warmth of his personality combined with his extensive scholarship to make him one of Scotland's most influential teachers. One of his pupils at Glasgow was Adam Smith. In both public and private life Hutcheson exhibited that benevolence which his moral philosophy describes as the object of our moral approval.

The relationship between philosophy and religion in Hutcheson's philosophy is of considerable importance. His liberalism in religion not only shocked many who heard his early sermons, but caused his prosecution for heresy by the Presbyterian Synod of Glasgow. It was charged that he taught, in opposition to the Westminster confession, that the standard of moral goodness was the promotion of the happiness of others and that we could have a knowledge of good and evil, without, and prior to a knowledge of God. That Hutcheson should have defended his religious position while occupying a chair at the University of Glasgow is the more remarkable if one remembers that although religion in Scotland was becoming more liberal, only a few years earlier, in 1697, a young man had been hanged for professing deism.

The letters exchanged between Hutcheson and Hume are both interesting and informative. It is evident that there were differences in their general approach to moral philosophy. Thus in one of his letters Hutcheson observed that Hume lacked a certain warmth in the cause of virtue. In his reply Hume maintained that this lack was intentional and that the method which he pursued in his moral philosophy was that of the anatomist rather than that of the painter.[3] Some years later Hume applied for the vacant chair of moral philosophy at Edinburgh. Popular opinion was against him and he failed to receive the appointment. Hume believed that Hutcheson had opposed his appointment to this position. It is conceivable that Hutcheson, in spite of his liberal temper, may have opposed the appointment because of Hume's agnosticism and what appeared to Hutcheson to be a lack of warmth. However, sufficient evidence that he did so is lacking.

No discussion of Hutcheson's philosophy can proceed without an awareness of parallel developments in the philosophy of Joseph Butler. Both began their careers with letters to Samuel Clarke which were critical of the latter's rationalistic theology. Both studied for the ministry and became clergymen. Both express a great indebtedness to Shaftesbury.

[3] J. Y. T. Greig, ed., *The Letters of David Hume* (2 vols.; Oxford: Clarendon Press, 1932), I, 32.

Both express a preference for the methods of observation and experiment in the investigation of the nature of morality. They even share philosophical opponents, namely, the egoists. In attempting to discover the extent of the influence of Hutcheson and Butler on each other, it is necessary to keep in mind the dates of publication of their major works. Butler, born in 1692, was two years older than Hutcheson. At the time of the publication of Butler's *Fifteen Sermons* in 1726, Hutcheson had already published the six letters to the *Dublin Journal* and also the *Inquiry*, all of which appeared in 1725. It is in the *Essay on the Nature and Conduct of the Passions,* published in 1728, that we first find signs of Butler's influence. Hutcheson, under this influence, altered his theory to reflect Butler's account of the passions and his treatment of conscience as an authoritative faculty which regulates and governs behavior.

Although Hutcheson is best known for the essays published during his residence in Dublin, he published a considerable number of works during his years in Glasgow. The tract entitled *Considerations on Patronages, addressed to the Gentlemen of Scotland* was published in 1735. Hutcheson's longest work, *A System of Moral Philosophy,* was published in 1755, nine years after his death in 1746. A preface is included which contains an account of Hutcheson's life and writings by his friend William Leechman. In spite of the late publication of this work it is really an intermediate work which may have been begun as early as 1734 or 1735. W. R. Scott suggests that as Hutcheson's thought developed in the *System,* he preferred to publish a series of short works rather than to attempt extensive revisions.[4] These short works were the *Philosophiae Moralis Institutio Compendiaria, Ethices et Jurisprudentiae Naturalis Elementa continens, Libri Tres* and the *Metaphysicae Synopsis Ontologiam et Pneumatologiam complectens,* both published in 1742. To this period belongs also the *Logicae Compendium,* a small logical text published in 1756. A rough translation of the *Philosophiae Moralis Institutio Compendiaria* was published in 1746 with the title *A Short Introduction to Moral Philosophy in Three Books; containing the Elements of Ethics and the Law of Nature.* In these Compends the influence of Aristotle seems stronger than before and, in general, there is an increased preoccupation with classical sources not only in ethics but in metaphysics. In fact, while reading Hutcheson and Hume it is well to keep in mind their great fondness for Cicero. Hutcheson's close acquaintance with the writings of Marcus Aurelius was due in part to the fact that during the summer of

---

[4] Scott, *Francis Hutcheson,* p. 115.

1741 he prepared the greater half of a new translation of the *Meditations* which was published in 1742.

After an illness lasting several months Hutcheson died in 1746, at the age of fifty-two.

The scope of this book will be limited rather severely to a consideration of certain problems which arise in Hutcheson's theory with respect to the relationship between his theory of motivation and his moral sense doctrine. More specifically, these problems have to do with the question as to how, on Hutcheson's theory, morality is practical, how it comes to guide or govern human behavior. Because of the limitations placed upon the scope of this book, there will be many important aspects of his theory – for example, his relationship to utilitarianism – which will not be considered in detail.

In extremely compressed form, some of the thoughts and arguments which are expressed in more orderly and detailed fashion in the course of this book might be outlined as follows: Hutcheson has long been associated with the attempt to show that morality is practical and dynamic. In this respect he is followed by Hume. Both are extremely critical of the rationalists in that the latter had failed to provide a plausible account of how the same reason which gave us knowledge of moral distinctions could also move us to action. In the *Inquiry Concerning Moral Good and Evil,* his earliest work dealing with moral philosophy, Hutcheson was concerned mainly with a exposition of his moral sense doctrine. His next work, the *Essay on the Nature and Conduct of the Passions and Affections,* represents an attempt to provide a theory of motivation. However, when Hutcheson's moral sense theory is conjoined with his theory of motivation the results are conceptually catastrophic. Puzzles and paradoxes appear as he struggles to explain how the moral sense influences motivation and how what he calls "justifying reasons" are related to action.

With this sketch of some of the main issues with which this book will be involved, it may be helpful to provide a brief indication of how these issues will be developed in ensuing chapters.

Chapter I will be devoted to a critical examination of Hutcheson's theory of motivation. Close attention will be given to the distinctions which he draws between passions, affections, and calm general desires. Two topics will be singled out for close study. The first of these is Hutcheson's refutation of egoism; the second, the "calm desires" doctrine and its relationship to Hutcheson's treatment of the place of reason in conduct.

Hutcheson's moral sense doctrine will be subjected to close study in Chapter II. This will lead to an exposition and evaluation of Hutcheson's theory concerning the analysis, nature, and function of moral judgments. The interpretations of Hutcheson's theory advanced by Broad, Frankena, and others will be discussed and assessed.

In Chapter III I shall attempt to substantiate my claim that a conceptual clash occurs when Hutcheson's theory of motivation is combined with his moral sense theory. Following an examination of Hutcheson's arguments against the rationalists, I shall present a detailed study of Hutcheson's own position concerning the problem of how moral judgments may influence to action and how obligation is related to motivation. It will be concluded that Hutcheson's position is in many respects untenable.

Chapter IV will be devoted to a brief consideration of how, in his later works, Hutcheson revised his moral sense theory.

Chapter V will present some concluding remarks. These will serve as a summary of specific suggestions made in earlier chapters as to how some of the difficulties inherent in the sort of theory held by Hutcheson might be avoided.

CHAPTER I

HUTCHESON'S THEORY OF MOTIVATION

THE ORIGINS AND DISTINCTIVE CHARACTERISTICS OF HUTCHESON'S THEORY OF MOTIVATION[1]

Hutcheson's theory of motivation constitutes one of his most valuable contributions to moral philosophy. If originality is taken to mean novelty, then Hutcheson's theory must be judged lacking in originality and highly derivative. Let us look at some sources of his doctrines. When he describes man's social nature and argues that benevolence is not reducible to self-love, he is much influenced by Shaftesbury. In his claim that reason provides no motive to action he invokes the authority of Aristotle. In his doctrine of the "calm desires" he was influenced, at one point or another, by Plato, Malebranche, and Butler. But if originality may mean not just novelty but freshness of insight in the treatment of materials, then Hutcheson is in this sense original. He presents challenging discussions of almost every issue that had been raised by writers concerned with the subject of motivation as related to moral philosophy. Moreover, his trenchant criticisms of psychological egoism and psychological hedonism must be ranked with those of Butler as among the most significant contributions to the history of ethics. Incidentally, it may be noted that many of Hutcheson's observations on the affections and passions had appeared in his *Inquiry Concerning Moral Good and Evil,* published in 1725, one year before the appearance of Butler's *Sermons* in 1726. Butler's influence

---

[1] A note is required in order to clarify references to Hutcheson's earlier works. The first of these is *An Inquiry into the Original of our Ideas of Beauty and Virtue, In Two Treatises I. Inquiry Concerning Beauty, Order, Harmony and Design, and II. Inquiry Concerning Moral Good and Evil.* I shall refer only to the second treatise, the *Inquiry Concerning Moral Good and Evil,* and shall refer to it as *Inquiry.* The latter is reproduced in L. A. Selby-Bigge's *British Moralists.* Because of the greater availability of Selby-Bigge's anthology, references to the *Inquiry* will be to its occurrence in Selby-Bigge. Selby-Bigge has reprinted the second edition, London, 1726. The second of Hutcheson's earlier works is *An Essay on the Nature and Conduct of the Passions and Affections, with Illustrations upon the Moral Sense.* My references will be to the fourth edition, London, 1756. This work is divided into two treatises. I shall refer to the first as *Essay* and to the second as *Illustrations.*

is evident in Hutcheson's *Essay,* published in 1728. However, as will be indicated, Hutcheson's arguments against psychological egoism raise points not discussed by Butler. Furthermore, as regards a comparison between these writers, Hutcheson's prolonged critique of ethical rationalism and his examination of the place of reason in morals have no parallel in Butler.

Seen in broad historical perspective, Hutcheson's theory of motivation, like most of his philosophy, may be said to carry forward the program of Locke's empiricism. It is in terms of such a program that the passions and affections are examined as the contents of a direct introspective awareness. Hutcheson's psychology is preoccupied with two themes which emerge from the materials of what Locke called "reflection." First, he complains continually that some "strange love of simplicity" has led many writers to overlook some of our simple perceptions. In order to account for these perceptions he argues for the existence of additional senses, notably a moral sense and a sense of beauty. Secondly, he maintains against the psychological egoists that if our affections were to be studied without preconceptions, they should be found to include benevolence, an ultimate desire for the happiness of others. Yet, there are many characteristics of Hutcheson's theory not found in Locke. Here, as at many points in Hutcheson's philosophy, it is Shaftesbury who adds his influence. In a famous letter to General Stanhope, Shaftesbury declares the doctrine of innate principles "one of the childishest disputes that ever was." He goes on to state what he believes to be the issue:

Not whether the very philosophical propositions about right and wrong were innate; but whether the passion or affection towards society was such; that is to say, whether it was natural and came of itself, or was taught by art, and was the product of a lucky hit of some first man who inspired and delivered down the prejudice.[2]

It is in Shaftesbury that we find an emphasis upon the fact that certain instincts, propensities, and appetites are natural to man and that many of these are social rather than egoistic in character.

With these comments upon some of the most general influences upon Hutcheson's extremely complex theory, let us turn to his theory itself, noting additional influences as they appear relevant. In my study of Hutcheson's moral philosophy, I shall be very much concerned with tracing the way in which he combines his doctrine of the moral sense

---

[2] *The Life, Unpublished Letters, and Philosophical Regimen of Anthony, Earl of Shaftesbury,* ed. by Benjamin Rand (London: Swann Sonnenschein & Co., Ltd., 1900), p. 415.

with other doctrines concerning motivation. It will therefore be of interest to keep in mind an overall view of how Hutcheson's philosophy developed in these respects. In early editions of his *Inquiry*, Hutcheson tends to make all topics subservient to his doctrine of the moral sense. He grants that "the motives of human actions, or their immediate causes, would be best understood after considering the passions and affections," but adds that "here we shall only consider the springs of the actions which we call virtuous, as far as it is necessary to settle the general foundation of the moral sense." [3] In the *Essay* he undertakes to supply a more complete examination of the nature of motivation. In the *System* and the *Short Introduction to Moral Philosophy*, both of which were published after the *Essay*, Hutcheson's discussions of the nature and function of the moral sense are always preceded by sections outlining his views concerning the passions and affections. It must be admitted, however, that the latter works add very little to Hutcheson's earlier discussions of psychological issues.

The terms "affections" and "passions" are rarely used in contemporary ethics. Because they are crucial to an appreciation of Hutcheson it is important to attend to his use of them. As regards the earlier history of these terms Wolfson remarks that "on the whole, mediaeval authors use these three terms *passio, affectus,* and *affectio,* synonymously." [4] In the seventeenth and eighteenth centuries many writers used the term "passion" in a very wide sense to include affections, impulses, appetites, and instincts of all sorts. Norman Kemp Smith makes the following statement:

"Passion" . . . is the term used by Hutcheson, as it is also used by Hume, to cover all types of feeling, not only feeling in the strict sense (i.e. pleasure and pain), but also the instinctive bodily appetites, the emotions and sentiments and in addition all the various types of appreciation which find expression in value-judgments.[5]

Although it is true that Hutcheson sometimes uses the term "passion" in this all-inclusive sense, it is of the utmost importance to insist that he also uses it in a more specific sense when he comes to draw careful distinctions between the various elements named by Kemp Smith. In this more specific sense, the passions are distinguished from the affections and from the pleasures and pains which have their source in the moral sense. Thus, for example, in the title *An Essay on the Conduct of the Passions and Affections* the terms "passions" and "affections" are not synonyms. The

[3] Selby-Bigge, *British Moralists,* I, 84.
[4] Harry Austryn Wolfson, *The Philosophy of Spinoza* (2 vols.; New York: Meridian Books, Inc., 1958), II, 193.
[5] Norman Kemp Smith, *The Philosophy of David Hume,* p. 44.

above statement by Kemp Smith is therefore most misleading and tends to equate Hutcheson's position as regards motivation with that of Hume, whereas the truth is that, in spite of their many points of agreement, there are significant differences between them. At the outset, it may be remarked that some of Hume's most famous phrases could not be ascribed to Hutcheson. Hume's term "calm passion" would, according to Hutcheson, involve a self-contradiction, since in the latter's terminology all passions are violent. Nor is Hutcheson likely to have used, or even approved, Hume's phrase "slave of the passions" as descriptive of the function of reason.

But let us proceed to clarify exactly what Hutcheson means by the terms "affections" and "passions." The term "affection" is used by Hutcheson to include: (1) desire and aversion; (2) certain other feelings such as joy, sorrow, or despair. These affections have one characteristic in common, namely, the fact that they all require previous perceptions of pleasure and pain. Unless I had previously experienced the pleasures of eating food, I should not, when hungry, desire to eat food. The feelings of joy and sorrow are, in Hutcheson's terms, "modifications of new states, arising from our apprehensions of objects or events as obtained or not obtained, according to our previous desire; or repelled and prevented, or not, according to our previous aversions." [6] For example, a person who has previously desired wealth will find joy in reflecting on riches which he has already received or which he expects to obtain. An invalid will feel sorrow in contemplating the return of a pain such as he has previously experienced.

Desire and aversion are the affections with which Hutcheson is mostly concerned, calling them at one point "the only pure affections in the strictest sense." [7] A comparison of Hutcheson's position with that of Locke is illuminating. In answer to the question as to what determines the will in regard to our actions, Locke makes the following statement:

... that, upon second thoughts, I am apt to imagine is not, as is generally supposed, the greater good in view, but some (and for the most part the most pressing) *uneasiness* a man is present under. This is that which successively determines the *will* and sets us upon those actions we perform. This *uneasiness* we may call, as it is, *desire*; which is an *uneasiness* of the mind for want of some absent good.[8]

As contrasted with Locke on this score, Hutcheson follows Malebranche

[6] Hutcheson, *Essay*, p. 60.
[7] *Ibid.*
[8] John Locke, *An Essay Concerning Human Understanding* (2 vols.; London: J. M. Dent & Sons, Ltd., 1961), I, 207.

in distinguishing between the spiritual affections and those bodily impulses and perturbations which are called "passions." Throughout the
Essay Hutcheson affirms that desire itself is a simple idea, entirely different from other ideas, especially pleasure and pain, which may frequently accompany it. And in the case of pure desire or aversion, no
uneasiness is present. Uneasiness is ascribed instead to the presence of
passions.

An important difference between the affections and passions must be
noted. Desire and aversion, unlike the passions, arise from some opinion
of good or evil to be obtained or avoided. By "good" or "natural good"
Hutcheson means "pleasure"; by "evil," pain. In the case of the passions,
on the other hand, no antecedent opinion of good or evil need be present
for their operation. Of his use of the term "passion" Hutcheson says:

When the word passion is imagined to denote anything different from the
affections, it includes a strong brutal impulse of the will, sometimes without
any distinct notions of good, public of private, attended with a confused
sensation either of pleasure or pain . . .[9]

Among the appetites named by Hutcheson are anger, hunger, thirst,
sexual urges, and the propensity to seek company, all of which are as
instinctive in their operation as are our tendencies to blink when a loud
noise occurs or to stretch out our arms when in danger of falling.

When an impulse or appetite is satisfied, the thought of this pleasurable
state gives rise to desire. Although Hutcheson no doubt believes that most
desires arise in exactly this way, he does not suppose that all desires do so.
And this is important. Desire may arise whenever there is a thought of
pleasure to be obtained. But many pleasures may be experienced in
circumstances in which we have no awareness of the characteristic uneasiness and distress of impulsive appetites. This is true of many of our
pleasures of sight, smell, hearing, and touch. And, more important for
Hutcheson's aesthetics and moral philosophy, this is true also of those
pleasures of the imagination which he ascribes to our sense of beauty and
our moral sense.

With these comments in mind, we may attempt to arrange in orderly
fashion the rather large number of terms which Hutcheson employs in
describing human behavior. There are, first of all, terms like "appetite,"
"instinct," and "propensity" as these are used to refer to those "springs
of action" which do not presuppose antecedent opinions of good or evil
in their objects. Sometimes Hutcheson refers even to these as kinds of
desire. For the most part, however, Hutcheson reserves the term "desire"

[9] Hutcheson, *Essay*, p. 28.

for situations in which desire is that which is excited by an antecedent opinion of good to be obtained. Most of such desires are not "pure." That is, they are accompanied with the cravings and perturbations of passion and as such are often referred to as "passionate desires." But not all desires are passionate. Some desires are calm and pure. These calm desires may be further divided into the particular and the general. Hutcheson does seem to think that there are calm particular desires. For example, he refers to the "calm desire of wealth" [10] and contrasts it with the passion of avarice. However, such references to calm particular desires are very rare. The only calm desires which he discusses at length are calm self-love and calm benevolence, both of which he calls "calm general desires."

These two calm desires, self-love and benevolence, are central to Hutcheson's theory. Both are described as calm, without uneasiness, general as opposed to the particular desires, and as being ultimate determinations of the will. These desires can never be excited by reason alone. Yet Hutcheson often refers to their operation as "rational appetite." By this he refers to what might be called the mediating function of cognition. That is, these desires are notable in that they are directed by reason to their long-range goals. Self-love is a calm desire which, unlike particular impulses, is directed towards the long-range happiness of the agent. Benevolence as a calm general desire seeks the "greatest good of the greatest number" a phrase, incidentally, which Hutcheson was one of the first to use in English ethics. Calm general benevolence is distinguished from benevolence as a particular and passionate propensity. Most important, Hutcheson maintains that the calm general desires may govern and restrain our particular passions. Although it is likely that he had read Butler in this connection, he never refers to the latter as the source of this doctrine, but instead, on several occasions, refers to the occurrence of this doctrine in Plato and Aristotle, notably in Book IX of Plato's *Republic*.

HUTCHESON'S REFUTATION OF EGOISM

In view of Hutcheson's almost incessant attacks upon the egoists, it is worth recalling briefly the nature of their theories. A great many of the controversies of seventeenth and early eighteenth century ethics may be viewed as commentaries on the so-called "selfish system" of Thomas Hobbes. The main outlines of Hobbes' argument are as follows: Hobbes contends, not only that all of our appetites are directed towards self-

[10] Francis Hutcheson, *A System of Moral Philosophy* (2 vols.; London: A. Millar, 1755), I., 12.

preservation, but also that those actions alone are reasonable which aim at self-preservation. As a result, Hobbes proceeds to explain how many motives and sentiments which appear to be social are really manifestations of self-interest. He then uses this analysis as a basis for his examination of political society. Beginning with a description of the ruthless egoism which man exhibits in the "state of nature," Hobbes maintains that political society owes its existence, not to social impulses, but to man's use of reason in creating the state as an instrument for his self-preservation. It was this "selfish system" which moved so many writers to construct ethical theories in conscious opposition to Hobbes. In such writers as Richard Cumberland opposition to Hobbes takes the form of a defense of the original and natural character of our social drives. In the works of Cambridge Platonists such as Ralph Cudworth and Henry More, Hobbes' system is opposed by an appeal to ethical truths which, like Plato's Forms, are eternal, immutable and gained through reason.

But all of the commentators on Hobbes were not detractors. Among Hobbes' most enthusiastic followers was Bernard de Mandeville. Mandeville's *Fable of the Bees* was one of the most widely discussed books of the eighteenth century. The complete title of Hutcheson's *Inquiry,* which was quoted earlier, indicates that it was a defense of Shaftesbury against Mandeville. In fact, there is hardly a work by Hutcheson in which space is not devoted to attacking Mandeville's cynical egoism. The subject matter of the *Fable* was not entirely original. Other writers had presented views not so very different from those pictured in the *Grumbling Hive* where public benefits, such as the arts, prosperity, commerce, and wealth, are the results of private vices such as fraud, envy, and self-interest. But Mandeville's exposition was extraordinarily clever and the weapons of satire, wit, and cynicism added much to the impact of his work.

Let us now turn to psychological egoism and Hutcheson's refutation of it. Psychological egoism is a theory which holds that the sole motive of all actions is a desire to do what the agent believes will most further his self-interest. A closely related theory is psychological hedonism according to which the sole motive of all actions is a desire to do what the agent believes will provide him with the greatest possible amount of pleasure. In thus conceiving psychological hedonism as a form of psychological egoism, we may note that, as Broad says, "psychological egoism might be true, even though psychological hedonism were false; but, if psychological egoism be false, psychological hedonism cannot be true." [11] Both

---

[11] C. D. Broad, *Ethics and the History of Philosophy* (New York: The Humanities Press, Inc., 1952), p. 219.

psychological hedonism and psychological egoism may be contrasted with ethical egoism, according to which everyone ought to act so as to maximize his self-interest. Those of Hutcheson's arguments which we shall be considering in the next sections of this chapter are directed against psychological egoism and psychological hedonism.

Arguments and observations relevant to his attack upon various types of egoism may be found throughout Hutcheson's works. However, there is one section early in his *Essay* which presents a sustained treatment of his most central arguments against the egoists. In this section he presents his views under four arguments and his conclusions from them. These arguments are somewhat compressed in character. In order to explicate them, it will be necessary to supplement them with background material from the remainder of the *Essay*.

Hutcheson's first pronouncement is as follows: "No desire of any event is excited by any view of removing the uneasy sensation attending this desire itself." [12] Let us reconstruct the sort of argument from which this follows as a conclusion. To do so, it is helpful to recall that he is considering the sort of position held by Locke. In his *Essay*, Locke had stated that desire "is an uneasiness of the mind for want of some absent good." [13] It is this uneasiness, according to Locke, which determines the will. How this takes place is not entirely clear. Locke appears to have held that an absent good raises an uneasiness which is painful. Wherever there is pain there is always desire joined to it and, in Locke's terms, desire is hardly distinguishable from this pain or uneasiness. This desire which is joined to uneasiness is a desire to get rid of the uneasiness .All desire is therefore really aversion to present pain.

Now there is no doubt that Locke's theory bears some relationship to the situations in which we use words like "desire," "aversion," "pleasure," and so on. Frequently enough we find in our experience some organic sensations such as the pangs of hunger whose painfulness is such that we want to rid ourselves of them. The connection between our pangs and our wanting to be rid of them may seem to introspection to be so close that we may sympathize with Locke's claim that desire is hardly distinguishable from this uneasy and painful state.

Sidgwick presents a wonderfully perceptive analysis of the difference between the pain which makes us want to be rid of it and what he calls desire proper. Sidgwick's point is as follows: In both the pain and desire we feel a stimulus prompting us to pass from the present state into a

---

[12] Hutcheson, *Essay*, p. 16.
[13] Locke, *Essay*, I, 207.

different one. In pain the stimulus is a negative "wanting to be rid of," whereas in desire proper the movement is a positive wanting of a future end.[14] Incidentally, it may be remarked that at several crucial points in his analysis of the nature of pleasure and desire Sidgwick indicates his indebtedness to Hutcheson. And, it may be added, the influence, in turn, of Sidgwick's arguments in these areas upon more recent writers such as Broad and Nowell-Smith is clearly distinguishable.

Using Sidgwick's terms, we may point out that Hutcheson marks a complete departure from those theories like Locke's which identified desire in terms of an "uneasiness" and a "wanting to be rid of." Hutcheson would agree with Sidgwick that desire proper is positive, not negative, a wanting of some future end, not just a wanting to be rid of an uneasiness. Desire, according to Hutcheson, is a simple idea, distinct from any sensation. Uneasiness accompanies many of our desires, but is not to be identified with them.[15] In summary, Hutcheson's position might be set forth as follows: When we hear someone say "I am thirsty" we may distinguish: (1) certain organic sensations which the speaker might locate in his throat, tongue, and stomach and which might be described as painful and uneasy; (2) a desire, not identifiable with these sensations and having as its object drink; (3) the satisfaction which would follow if the object in question were to be obtained. It would then be an error to identify the desire for drink with the organic sensations. Moreover, the organic sensations which accompany a desire cannot arouse the desire itself.

From this account of desire Hutcheson concludes that "the uneasy sensation accompanying and connected with the desire itself, cannot be a motive to that desire which it presupposes." Or, as he announces at the beginning of this section, "no desire of any event is excited by any view of removing the uneasy sensation attending this desire itself." [16]

A somewhat parallel argument is presented by Hutcheson to show that no desire is excited by the expectation of obtaining the pleasure arising from the gratification of that desire itself. His argument is no doubt directed against the hedonist who wants to convince us that all desire is for pleasure. Such a hedonist would have us believe that although people claim to desire money, fame, and all sorts of things, what they really desire is the pleasure which accrues from the attainment of these objects. If Hutcheson is correct, such a hedonist is misrepresenting the character

[14] Henry Sidgwick, *The Methods of Ethics* (2nd ed.; London: Macmillan and Co., 1877), p. 39.
[15] Hutcheson, *Essay*, p. 44.
[16] *Ibid.*, p. 16.

of desire and pleasure. According to Hutcheson, the pleasures of satisfying our desires presuppose the existence of the very desires which are
directed upon some object or event other than pleasure. Hutcheson adds
an ingenious observation to the effect that if desires could be aroused with
the view of obtaining the joys of their own gratification, then the most
fantastic desires could be aroused. For example, I should be able to arouse
in myself intense desires for smoking Turkish cigars, for bathing in cognac,
for eating raw mushrooms, etc. just by the thought of the pleasures which
would be gained if I were to have and to gratify these desires. As we might
put it, it is a logical truth that one cannot have the satisfaction resulting
from gratifying a desire unless one really does have and does gratify that
desire. Similarly, it is logically impossible for a desire to have as its object
its own gratification.

The remaining three arguments which Hutcheson sets forth in that part
of the *Essay* under consideration share a main purpose which is to show
that benevolence can not be treated as a special case of self-love.

The point which Hutcheson makes in the first of these arguments may
be brought out by close attention to the argument which I should put as
follows: Self-love raises a desire for whatever will bring happiness to us.
But the desire for the happiness of others would, if satisfied, be a source
of happiness to us. Therefore self-love may raise a desire-for-a-desire-for
the happiness of others. Notice that the conclusion is not simply that self-
love raises a desire for the happiness of others. As Hutcheson points out,
no act of volition can raise a desire in us. In particular, self-love cannot of
itself create a real and ultimate desire for the happiness of others. Because
of the prospects of advantage, honor, self-approbation, rewards from God,
etc. we may desire to have or wish that we had certain desires. But, again,
desires are not raised solely by wishing to have them. Otherwise we could
be bribed to love, hate, pity, etc. Consequently, benevolence, a regard for
the welfare of others, cannot be raised in us through self-love simply by
the desire to be benevolent.

In the second of the sections dealing with the relationship between
self-love and benevolence, Hutcheson makes the following claim: "There
are in men desires of the happiness of others, when they do not conceive
this happiness as the means of obtaining any sort of happiness to themselves." [17] Hutcheson goes on to remark on the distinction between subordinate and ultimate desires and defends himself against those who might
claim that although desires for the happiness of others do exist, these are
subordinate to ultimate desires for our own happiness. He concedes that

[17] *Ibid.,* p. 20.

there are cases in which for example, business partners may wish for the happiness of each other primarily because of self-interest. However he claims that there is benevolence which is ultimate and not reducible to self-love and that it is this ultimate benevolence which is approved as virtuous. In such claims that benevolence does exist, Hutcheson is not presenting an argument so much as pointing to what he believes to be a fact, verifiable through experience, which the egoist has distorted or ignored.

Hutcheson now asks the following question: "May not our benevolence be at least a desire of the happiness of others, as the means of obtaining the pleasure of the public sense, from the contemplation of their happiness?" [18] Again this question concerns the attempts which are made to show that desires for the welfare of others are instances of what is only subordinate good will, i.e. a good will which is ultimately self-regarding. This question, however, is of specific interest in that it centers around the role of sympathy, a concept which was to be of considerable importance in the moral philosophies of David Hume and Hutcheson's illustrious pupil, Adam Smith. In the *Essay*, Hutcheson uses the term "public sense" as a synonym for what he refers to in the *System* and elsewhere as "sympathy." The public sense is defined as "our determination to be pleased with the happiness of others, and to be uneasy at their misery." [19] The public sense functions in the following manner: (1) we obtain opinions of the happiness or unhappiness of others; (2) these opinions give rise to pleasures or pains in us. It is important to note that "sympathy" or the "public sense" is not a passion. Nor does the belief alone that others are happy or unhappy ever raise a passion in us. Here as elsewhere, belief by itself never moves to action. However beliefs concerning the feelings and welfare of others may arouse sympathetic pleasures or pains in us and these in turn may excite us to desire or aversion.

It is at this point that Hutcheson would insist upon the fact that the desires excited by sympathy are not to be identified with those of benevolence. He presents two lines of argument in supporting his case. In the first place, he points out that the pains of compassion may be relieved by a direct attempt to aid the person in distress, an attempt prompted by benevolence. Yet such pains might also be relieved by turning one's mind from the distressing situation or by taking an opiate to forget it. And if all goodwill were truly subordinate to self-love, the latter would be as much approved as the former. In the second place, Hutcheson presents ex-

[18] *Ibid.*, p. 21.
[19] *Ibid.*, p. 5.

amples and observations designed to illustrate the disproportion which often exists between our benevolence and our anticipation of sympathetic pleasures. He claims, plausibly in my opinion, that we do often try to relieve the suffering of others even when our sympathetic feelings are mostly painful. He presents for consideration the case of the dying man who, Hutcheson claims ,retains his desires for the welfare of others even though, because of his immanent death, their subsequent welfare could not afford him sympathetic pleasure. And he refers to cases of love, parental affection, and patriotism in which the object intended does not seem to be the future pleasures of sympathy. It would therefore be both logically and psychologically possible for a desire to promote the good of others to move an agent even at times during which he experienced or anticipated no sympathetic feelings whatsoever. Consider Boswell's self-portrait: "I own, Sir, I have not so much feeling for the distress of others as some people have or pretend to have, but I know this that I would do all in my power to relieve them." [20]

In short, Hutcheson's theory, while recognizing the importance of sympathy, is careful to distinguish between its role and that of benevo-lence. It may be noted in passing that Hume's position in his *Treatise* places great stress upon the role of sympathy, whereas in his *Enquiry Concerning the Principles of Morals* he returns to a position closer to that of Hutcheson as regards the treatment of sympathy and benevolence.

In taking stock of Hutcheson's arguments against the egoists one is reminded of the story about the proverbial little old lady who complained that Shakespeare's *Hamlet* was, after all, so full of quotations which one has heard before. It is in a sense a tribute to Hutcheson that a reader who knows his Sidgwick, Broad, and Nowell-Smith will find in Hutcheson earlier statements of positions concerning motivation with which he has become familiar. Nor, as I have claimed, is this an accident. Hutcheson was widely read in his lifetime and his views exerted a great influence on many later writers. As we survey his treatment of desire and its objects we see that he has presented a serious if not devastating challenge to the sort of views held by Locke on desire and to the egoists who attempted to reduce benevolence to self-love. Finally, his analysis of the character and role of sympathy is perceptive and is of interest as one compares his view with that of Hume or Adam Smith.

---

[20] James Boswell, *Boswell's Life of Johnson,* ed. by George B. Hill (6 vols.; Oxford: The Clarendon Press, 1934-50), II, 469.

A reader who has followed Hutcheson's arguments against the egoists has surely received the impression that psychological hedonism is false, that pleasure is not the object of desire. Such a reader may turn with puzzlement to those many passages in Hutcheson's theory of motivation which appear to place an extraordinary emphasis on pleasure and pain. And, in order to appreciate how his theory of motivation is related to his moral sense doctrine, it is indeed necessary to concentrate further on his use of the terms "desire," "aversion," "pleasure," and "pain."

We might begin with a somewhat naive observation to the effect that the frequency with which Hutcheson uses the terms "pleasure" and "pain" does not in itself make him a hedonist. After all, Aristotle, who is no hedonist, spends a good deal of time talking about pleasure.

But how are we to explain those many passages in which Hutcheson sets forth a list of the senses and then proceeds to list the desires for the various pleasures of these senses. The following passage is typical:

Desires arise in our mind, from the frame of our nature, upon apprehension of good or evil in objects, actions, or events, to obtain for ourselves or others the agreeable sensation, when the object or event is good; or to prevent the uneasy sensation, when it is evil.[21]

One wonders nervously whether Hutcheson does not slip backwards at times into hedonism. Does he not write at times as if he held that many of our desires are for pleasure?

In reply, it must be granted that his treatment of those explanations which employ appeals to pleasure and pain is far from unequivocal. However, certain comments are called for which may aid in clarifying his position. To begin with, it is necessary to recall that according to Hutcheson pleasures and pains appear in various contexts. Take, for example, the pleasures which are derived from the gratifying of some appetite or "passion." With regard to these, Hutcheson holds tenaciously to the view that desire is directed towards objects, not towards pleasure. But there are other situations in which pleasures and desires occur. As we noted earlier, many pleasures may occur in situations preceded by no occurrence of passionate appetites. "No man is distressed," Hutcheson says, "for want of fine smells, harmonious sounds, beautiful objects, wealth, power, or grandeur, previously to some opinion formed of these things as good, or some prior sensation of their pleasures." [22] Nor is there an appetite or

[21] Hutcheson, *Essay*, p. 7.
[22] *Ibid.*, p. 92.

passion toward virtue. In the case of these pleasures which are not preceded by passions is desire directed towards pleasure? At one point Hutcheson says, as we quoted him above, that desire arises to obtain the "agreeable sensation." Yet in other passages he rejects the theory that virtue is pursued because of the concomitant pleasure. The latter theory, he had maintained in the *Inquiry*, "plainly supposes a sense of virtue antecedent to ideas of advantage, upon which this advantage is founded." [23] As we shall see later, no one could be more insistent than Hutcheson in holding that the pleasures of virtuous action cannot be the end of desire, for these pleasures can only be obtained by aiming at an object, that object being, in his opinion, the good of others aimed at by benevolence. In short, it must be granted that Hutcheson is inconsistent in his statements about the objects of desire. However, it may be added that at the most crucial points in his theory he never fails to insist that desire is directed towards objects other than pleasure.

In clarifying Hutcheson's position in these respects it may be helpful to introduce some distinctions drawn by G. E. Moore. In his *Principia Ethica* Moore argues at length that when it is held that desire is always "*because of* some pleasure," the latter expression may have two different meanings. According to the one, the pleasure is the *object* of desire; according to the other it is the *cause* of desire, but not its object.[24] Moore contends, further, that whereas pleasure may quite possibly be the *cause* of desire, the hedonists are mistaken in holding that it is the *object* of desire.

Hutcheson's position would have gained greatly in clarity and consistency if he had observed the sort of distinctions to which Moore draws attention. As it is, Hutcheson's views concerning the objects of desire cannot be made consistent. Nevertheless, it may be claimed that he returns constantly to a position, in agreement with Moore, that pleasure is not the object of desire, but is somehow the cause of it. This sort of interpretation of Hutcheson is adopted by Norman Kemp Smith. The latter states that "pleasure and pain, for Hume as for Hutcheson, are merely the efficient causes, not the objects or ends of action." [25] To the extent that the views of Hutcheson and Hume may be treated together as regards these issues it may be remarked in passing that this interpretation is also in fundamental agreement with E. B. McGilvary's influential article,[26]

[23] Selby-Bigge, *British Moralists*, I, 92.
[24] George Edward Moore, *Principia Ethica* (Cambridge: The University Press, 1948), p. 69.
[25] Norman Kemp Smith, *The Philosophy of David Hume*, p. 164.
[26] E. B. McGilvary, "Altruism in Hume's *Treatise*," *Philosophical Review*, XII, No. 3 (1903), 275-95.

to which Kemp Smith expresses indebtedness, and with the interpretation of F. C. Sharp.[27] By contrast, it is in sharp disagreement with the interpretation of Hutcheson and Hume found in T. H. Green. Perhaps as a consequence of a failure to take the whole of Hutcheson's theory into account, Green attributes to Hutcheson the position that pleasure is the object of all desire.[28]

If we adopt the sort of interpretation of Hutcheson advanced by Kemp Smith and consistent with the distinctions made by G. E. Moore, then certain curious questions remain with respect to the nature of pleasure and desire. Let us see how these questions arise in the context of Moore's discussion. Moore is led by the distinction between the object and cause of desire to make a further distinction between the "thought of a pleasure" and a "pleasant thought," a distinction not always clear in Hutcheson. Moore's theory is that in the case, for example, of drinking a glass of wine, "the *idea* of the drinking causes a feeling of pleasure in my mind, which helps to produce that state of incipient activity, which is called 'desire.' " [29] That is, it is a "pleasant thought" and not a "thought of pleasure" which produces desire. And, as productive of desire, Moore maintains that this pleasure may indeed "cause our desire or move us to action, but it is not our end or object nor our motive." [30] Notice, therefore, that Moore distinguishes between a "pleasant thought" which causes and moves us to action, yet which is not a motive. We have here a knotty but familiar terminological problem. Of the term "motive" Ralph Barton Perry says: "the first step toward clarification of its meaning is to distinguish between 'motive' in the specific sense applicable to human conduct, and 'motive' in the generalized sense applicable to whatever generates motion." [31] But now if we adopt a terminology according to which pleasure is a cause of desire but not a motive, then the question arises as to whether desire, which is certainly a motive for Hutcheson, is also a cause of action.

In arriving at the latter question we have come to a point where we shall want to make some general and synoptic observations concerning Hutcheson's theory and the roles played by terms like "desire," "aversion," and "pleasure" in explanation of behavior. But such observations had best

---

[27] Frank Chapman Sharp, *Ethics* (New York: The Century Co., 1928), p. 348.
[28] Thomas Hill Green, "Introduction to the Moral Part of Hume's 'Treatise,' " in *Works of Thomas Hill Green,* ed. by R. L. Nettleship, I (London: Longmans, Green, and Co., 1906), 321.
[29] Moore, *Principia Ethica,* p. 69.
[30] *Ibid.,* p. 70.
[31] Ralph Barton Perry, *Realms of Value* (Cambridge, Mass.: Harvard University Press, 1954), p. 44.

be postponed until we have given closer attention to what is perhaps the most important part of Hutcheson's theory of motivation, namely, his "calm desires" doctrine.

THE CALM DESIRES

Let us attend to some of the sources from which Hutcheson draws in the development of the "calm desires" doctrine. Hutcheson refers repeatedly to Malebranche. The latter had described two sorts of "springs of action." The first, which Malebranche calls "inclinations" have their source in God and may be subdivided into the following: (1) inclinations directed toward good in general; (2) inclinations directed toward our own welfare; (3) inclinations directed toward the good of others. It is a characteristic of inclinations that they would exist even if agents were pure spirits independent of the conditions of physical existence. The second kind of "spring of action" Malebranche refers to as "affections" or "passions." These are the instinctive appetites and impulses which Malebranche regards as agitations occurring through the disturbances of the "animal spirits." [32] Hutcheson adapts some of these features of Malebranche's theory to his own uses. His distinction between the calm desires and the passions parallels the distinction in kind which Malebranche draws between what he calls the "inclinations" and the "passions." Furthermore, Malebranche's treatment of spiritual determinations as independent of our physical existence is reflected in Hutcheson's use of the term "desire" to denote a simple idea distinguishable from all of the uneasiness of passion. Let it be noted emphatically, therefore, that Hutcheson could not possibly follow Hume in the latter's references to "calm passions." For Hutcheson, the term "calm passion" would be self-contradictory. Passions are always uneasy and agitated in Hutcheson's terminology.

When Hutcheson comes to discuss the manner in which our calm desires may govern or restrain our passions, he refers on two occasions to Book IX of Plato's *Republic*. The relevant passage in Book IX is no doubt that passage in which Socrates is discussing the division of the soul into three principles and the manner in which the lower principles, the "appetitive" and the "spirited," may be governed by the higher principle, reason. [33] Hutcheson's calm desires doctrine was undoubtedly influenced

[32] Nicholas Malebranche, *Treatise Concerning the Search After Truth*, trans. by T. Taylor (London: L. Lichfield, 1694), p. 150.
[33] Plato *The Republic*, in *The Dialogues of Plato*, trans. by B. Jowett (2 vols.; New York: Random House, 1937), I, 829.

also by Butler. This doctrine receives little emphasis in Hutcheson's *Inquiry*. It is in the *Essay*, which appeared in 1728 after Hutcheson had read Butler's *Sermons*, that Hutcheson began to emphasize this doctrine. In evaluating Hutcheson's position, however, it is fair to point out that he attempted a far more thoroughgoing analysis of this doctrine than Butler had provided.

Before entering upon a more critical examination of Hutcheson's calm desires doctrine let us consider its main features. Hutcheson follows the program of Locke in tracing the origins of our knowledge in sensation and reflection. Desire is therefore described as originating in reflection and as the sort of experience of which we have a direct introspective awareness. We have a simple idea of desire, an idea distinguishable from any of the uneasy sensations which may be concomitant with it. Desire and aversion are described as "two calm primary motions of the will." They are "the only pure affections in the strictest sense." [34]

If desire itself is, properly speaking, "calm" and "pure," what are we to make of the passages in which Hutcheson refers to "passionate desires" and even to the appetites as "desires"? If we examine his view with care we find that there are certain instinctive drives or impulses which are accompanied by uneasy, painful sensations. These are the appetites which do not depend for their existence on any previous opinions of good or evil in objects. These include hunger, thirst, sexual attraction, and, notably, benevolence. Contrasted with these appetites are those desires which depend for their existence upon prior perceptions of pleasure and pain, i.e. upon opinions of good and evil to be obtained or avoided. To be consistent, therefore, Hutcheson's view must be that desire, although it is itself a simple idea distinguishable from all uneasiness, often arises in a situation in which there has been prior appetite plus satisfaction of that appetite. This being the case, our desire is likely to be attended with some of the raw feel of instinct and may in that case be called a "passionate desire."

Such passionate desires, however, are held to be distinct from the will. That is, they are not the sort of desires which emerge from reflective choice. There are, therefore, desires which are not passionate, which arise following opinions of good or evil to be obtained or avoided, and which do not depend upon the prior existence of appetites. In our delight and desire for fine smells, harmonious sounds, beautiful objects, virtue, and honor we are not conscious of any pre-existing appetite or drive. Such desires, therefore, may be called "calm" and "pure."

[34] Hutcheson, *Essay*, p. 60.

I should suppose that it is desires of the latter sort that Hutcheson refers to, rather infrequently, as particular calm desires. This brings us to his distinction between particular and general desires. We find Hutcheson referring to "general calm desires" or "calm natural determinations." There are two such calm general desires, namely, calm benevolence and self-love. Calm extensive benevolence is to be contrasted with impulsive benevolence. Calm self-love employs the raw materials of appetite which contribute indirectly to self-love in that we cannot maximize our happiness without satisfying our particular appetites. These calm general desires are described as being directed by reason to their objects. Furthermore, the calm general desires are capable of commanding, governing or restraining the particular passions. Calm benevolence may lead us to take an extensive view as to what is for the welfare of others as opposed to the narrow view dictated by particular benevolent impulses. Similarly, self-love follows long-range views of what is to our interest. In doing so, it may restrain or redirect impulses or, in some cases, it may support the claims of some impulse such as our bodily need for sleep against the claims of some other impulse such as our need to obtain food.

Ryle has commented as follows concerning the calm desires doctrine:

Hume, following Hutcheson, was partially alive to this distinction between inclinations and agitations, when he noticed that some "passions" are intrinsically calm, while others are violent. He noticed too that a calm passion might "vanquish" a violent passion. But his antithesis of "calm" and "violent" suggests a mere difference of degree between two things of the same kind.[35]

Ryle is quite right in pointing out that Hume's antithesis, described above, suggests a difference of degree, not of kind. It must be insisted, however, that for Hutcheson the antithesis between calm desires and violent passions is quite clearly a difference between two things of different kinds. This is abundantly clear from the many passages in which he argues that affections may be distinguished from passions and that desire may exist without the uneasiness of passion. It is interesting to note in passing that Hutcheson's distinction between the calm desires and the passions is in many respects parallel to Ryle's distinction between what he calls "inclinations" and "agitations."

THE PLACE OF REASON IN CONDUCT

The calm desires doctrine is in part intended as an answer to those

[35] Gilbert Ryle, *The Concept of Mind* (New York: Barnes & Noble, Inc., 1949), p. 24.

rationalists such as Samuel Clarke who claimed that reason can be a motive to action. Hutcheson's repeated references to Aristotle leave no doubt that he considered himself a follower of Aristotle as regards the latter's view of the place of reason in conduct. A comparison of their views will therefore contribute to an understanding of Hutcheson's position.

In briefest outline, Aristotle may be described as dividing the desires into three species: appetite (epithumia); passion (thumos); and wish (boulesis). This is a division reminiscent of Plato's tripartite division of the soul. The basis for the division seems to rest mostly in the distinction between rational and non-rational desires. Appetite is the sort of desire which is unresponsive to reason. Passion is partly responsive to reason, partly not. Wish is the sort of desire which is responsive to and guided by reason.[36]

By comparison, we have already followed in detail Hutcheson's description of the calm desires which are guided by reason and the impulsive passions which are entirely without forethought of good or evil. Hutcheson usually makes his classification twofold between calm desires and passionate desires. Actually, he might, parallel to Aristotle, make a threefold distinction between calm desires which are guided by reason, passionate desires, which although they follow reason are to some extent turbulent and appetitive in being accompanied by violent sensations, and the appetites or passions which operate without any forethought of good or evil.

Aristotle distinguishes movement – the sort of behavior which might include reaction to a sensation – and action whose origin is choice. Choice, in turn, he declares to have its origin in desire and reasoning with a view to an end.[37] In a much-quoted passage, he goes on to say:

This is why choice cannot exist either without reason and intellect or without a moral state; for good action and its opposite cannot exist without a combination of intellect and character. Intellect itself however moves nothing . . .[38]

And, as Aristotle has maintained earlier in an equally famous passage, "we deliberate not about ends but about means." [39]

Each of these passages is referred to at one time or another by Hutcheson. They would reinforce the position which he himself adopts and

---

[36] Aristotle *Nichomachean Ethics,* trans. by W. D. Ross, in *The Basic Works of Aristotle,* ed. by Richard McKeon (New York: Random House, 1941), p. 968.
[37] *Ibid.,* p. 1024.
[38] *Ibid.*
[39] *Ibid.,* p. 970.

ascribes to Aristotle that reason alone does not provide the ends of action. As early as the *Inquiry,* Hutcheson presents the outlines of his position as regards reason. "What is reason," he asks, "but that sagacity we have in prosecuting any end?" [40] He goes on to maintain that reason judges the tendencies of actions and that ends are given, not by reason, but by affections and passions. The following passage is typical of his statement of this main theme, first begun in the *Inquiry* and developed in each subsequent work:

... about the ultimate ends there is no reasoning. We prosecute them by some immediate disposition or determination of the soul, which in the order of action is always prior to all reasoning; as no opinion or judgment can move to action where there is no prior desire of some end.[41]

But, keeping in mind the comparisons we have been making between Aristotle and Hutcheson, a difficulty arises through the fact that a number of recent commentators, including J. J. Walsh, D. J. Allan and G. E. M. Anscombe, have maintained that the foregoing outline of Aristotle's conception of practical reason is an oversimplification or distortion resulting from taking certain passages out of context. Their suggestions as to an adequate interpretation of Aristotle are by no means identical. Walsh, influenced by Allan, suggests the name "double-version" theory for a view which he claims is supported by recent scholarship. With respect to this "double-version" theory he states:

According to it, practical reason has two functions. In addition to the function of discovering and organizing the means to gain an end, it also has a function in the determination of ends themselves. This is the function of knowing general moral rules and applying them to particular cases.[42]

He refers to the first as the means-end function and the additional function he names the rule-example function. By the rule-example function Walsh means that function, as he later explains, "which is associated with wish and which determines the end through the application of rules to examples." [43] He cites a number of passages from Aristotle which are difficult to interpret on the single version of practical reasoning. The following is one of the more famous of such passages:

If excellence in deliberation is one of the traits of men of practical wisdom, we may regard this excellence as correct perception of that which conduces to the end, whereof practical wisdom is a true judgment.[44]

[40] Selby-Bigge, *British Moralists,* I, 115.
[41] Hutcheson, *System,* I, 38.
[42] James Jerome Walsh, *Aristotle's Conception of Moral Weakness* (New York: Columbia University Press, 1963), p. 131.
[43] *Ibid.,* p. 134.
[44] Aristotle *Nicomachean Ethics,* p. 1031.

In a recent article entitled "Thought and Action in Aristotle," G. E. M. Anscombe lends support to the double-version theory, although her description of the functions of practical reason in Aristotle differs considerably from Walsh's rule-example function. Anscombe grants that practical reason has a means-end function. But she argues that technical deliberation in the sense of practical cleverness in bringing particular situations about, does not constitute the entirety of choice. She points out that Aristotle "denies the name of 'choice' to the technical or executive decision, even though this is the fruit of deliberation, if that particular thing for the sake of which this decision is being made is not itself decided upon by deliberation." [45] And, as I understand her interpretation of Aristotle, the latter sort of deliberation concerns "living well in general." She suggests that rational wanting should be explained in terms of "what is wanted being wanted *qua* conducive to or part of 'doing well,' or blessedness." [46]

I shall not attempt to evaluate further these theories having to do with the correct interpretation of Aristotle. They seem to me to have considerable plausibility. What is of interest, however, in turning to Hutcheson, is that they render us alert to a certain framework of questions which need to be asked of his theory.

Is Hutcheson, then, an exponent of a single-version theory or of a double-version theory? Let us begin by examining the evidence which suggests the former alternative. It seems that all of Hutcheson's interpreters have regarded him as a predecessor of Hume in holding some form of the single-version theory which limits reason to what Walsh calls the means-end function. For example, Norman Kemp Smith maintains that "what chiefly influenced Hume was . . . [Hutcheson's] inversion of the roles ordinarily ascribed to passion and to reason respectively." [47] Further, he goes on to describe the role of reason in Hutcheson's theory as limited to the discovery of the means to the fulfillment of ends which have been dictated by the passions.

Oft-repeated statements in Hutcheson himself support the sort of single-version theory which Rachael Kydd refers to in connection with Hume as the doctrine of reason as the "mediate" or "oblique" cause of action.[48] What the latter theory means in the case of Hutcheson is this: Reason

[45] G. E. M. Anscombe, "Thought and Action in Aristotle," in *New Essays on Plato and Aristotle*, ed. by Renford Bambrough (London: Routledge & Kegan Paul, 1965), p. 146.

[46] *Ibid.*, p. 155.

[47] Norman Kemp Smith, *The Philosophy of David Hume*, p. 44.

[48] Rachael M. Kydd, *Reason and Conduct in Hume's Treatise* (New York: Russell & Russell Inc., 1964), p. 115.

may show us the tendencies of our actions. To act "reasonably" is to consider the various actions in our power, to form true opinions of them, and then to choose that course of action to which our passions and affections must incline us. Reasons or truths may show us that some ends are subordinate to more ultimate ends. They cannot alone make us desire any ends whatsoever. Hume is but repeating this doctrine of Hutcheson's when he presents his view as to the two ways in which reason can influence our conduct, namely "either when it excites a passion by informing us of the existence of something which is a proper object of it; or when it discovers the connection of causes and effects, so as to afford us means of exerting any passion." [49] Defenders of the above doctrine of reason as the oblique or mediate cause of action have insisted quite rightly that this role of reason is by no means negligible.

The question arises, whatever terminology we accept, whether the doctrine regarding the place of reason which we have ascribed to Hutcheson represents his entire position. Are there any indications that this is not all that needs to be said?

Let us examine in this connection, Rachael Kydd's arguments which seek to establish that these are practical judgments which prompt passions and that Hume holds this view. I shall want to ask at the same time whether or not these arguments apply equally well to Hutcheson. Earlier in her book, Kydd describes those portions of Hume's theory which have to do with how judgments may *direct* passions, as in the case of judgments about means to ends. Such a view would be what I have referred to earlier as a single-function interpretation of the place of reason. Her claim that reason also prompts passions would introduce an additional function of reason. She puts the question as follows:

Can we make practical judgments which prompt passions, i.e. judgments about what it would be necessary for us to do on reflection in view of the intrinsic nature of the actions open to us and our own instinctive dispositions? [50]

Such a practical judgment would be of the form "since x has the properties a b c . . . I must, on contemplating the fact that it has these properties, desire to do it." [51] Her view is that since Hume allows that there are passions founded on a distant view and reflection he should really also admit that there are practical promptive judgments. On her interpretation, when I judge that some object or other would be conducive

[49] Hume, *Treatise*, p. 459.
[50] Kydd, *Reason and Conduct*, p. 129.
[51] *Ibid.*, p. 130.

to my long-range interests, this must arouse or prompt a desire on my part to obtain it.

I believe this to be an erroneous interpretation of both Hutcheson and Hume. However, let us restrict ourselves to examining this interpretation if it were to be applied to Hutcheson. According to the latter, the fact that reason informs us of a distant view is not sufficient to move us to action. Some instinct, passion or affection is required. And, as a matter of fact, Hutcheson believes that there is a calm desire which follows the guidance of reason. Presumably, this is a matter of fact, contingent and, contrary to Kydd, not necessary. No judgment about our long-range interests can necessitate that a desire should arise. Hence Kydd's suggestion that practical reason can not only direct but prompt a passion is indefensible if applied to Hutcheson and also, I suspect, if applied to Hume.

We must conclude therefore that there is no evidence for ascribing to Hutcheson any sort of double-version theory, as Walsh calls it, of the function of reason. Reason is strictly limited to its means-end function. What needs to be emphasized is that although reason is thus restricted, Hutcheson appeals to a kind of desire which requires a most extraordinary description, namely, his calm general desire. It might be pointed out that, very broadly speaking, some of the functions ascribed to reason by the rationalists, become, on Hutcheson's theory, the functions of the calm desires. It is now calm desire which moves us towards a distant view of reflection. It is calm desire which is described as calm *general* desire, by which he suggests that it is the sort of motive which sides with principles rather than with isolated impulses. Indeed, to parody Hume, we might suggest that Hutcheson's considered doctrine is that reason is and ought to be the slave of the calm general desires.

Nowell-Smith presents an objection to the sort of position we have been considering. Commenting on the relationship of self-love to the particular passions, he makes the following statement:

... some philosophers have thought it possible to prove that we ought to follow what Butler calls "cool self-love" rather than "particular passions." But this must be a mistake; for to say this is to make a *moral* judgment, to side with the "calm" against the "violent" passions and to recommend people to follow their long-term interests rather than do what they happen to want to do at the moment. And these decisions and injuncions cannot, as Hume noticed, follow from the empirical statement that *if* a man is to pursue his long-term interests satisfactorily he must curb his passions.[52]

[52] P. H. Nowell-Smith, *Ethics* (London: Penguin Books, 1954), p. 229.

Is Hutcheson, then, making a moral judgment in siding with the calm as against the particular passions? I think not. At least not at this point in his theory. Later, we may find that he does make moral judgments which do side with the calm general desires. At this point in his theory Hutcheson is simply maintaining that our long-range interests in our own welfare may command our particular passions, even if this command is sometimes insufficiently strong to induce submission. In maintaining, further, that we ought to follow self-love, a calm general desire, rather than a particular passion, Hutcheson is claiming, as he states elsewhere, that, in one sense of the word "ought," to say that one is obliged to an action means "that the action is necessary to obtain happiness to the agent, or to avoid misery." [53] As Nowell-Smith himself maintains, "the language of 'ought' in so far as it is necessarily and intimately connected with *rules,* is appropriate to the achievement of long-term interests and not to the satisfaction of desires." [54]

But, to attend again to the last part of the earlier quotation from Nowell-Smith, would Hutcheson disagree with Hume's observation that decisions to side with calm desires cannot follow from the empirical statement that *if* a man is to pursue his long-term interests satisfactorily he must curb his passions? Again, I think not. Hutcheson would no doubt agree that nothing follows from this empirical statement. Furthermore, Hutcheson would agree with Hume that it is not contrary to reason as such to prefer a lesser good to a greater. But Hutcheson would insist that it is contrary to the command which the calm general desires issue to the passions, a command or constraint which is also a part of our nature and which is reflected in one sense of our use of the word "obligation." To prefer a lesser good to a greater is to act contrary to general inclinations, to long-term interests. And why ought I to follow my long-range interests? To this question, Hutcheson might retort that we do speak of being obliged in the sense, previously explained, in which we find that our calm general self-love exerts a command over particular impulses. He might add, further, that it is still entirely possible to inquire from a moral point of view whether any act prompted by calm self-love is morally obligatory.

As we observe Hutcheson's treatment of the various passions and affections, we can discern his fondness for conceiving of human nature as a constitution or organization in which some elements are subservient to others. In this respect he follows Shaftesbury and Butler. Hume, it might be added, is wary and even skeptical of this conception, as is shown, for

[53] Hutcheson, *Illustrations,* p. 232.
[54] Nowell-Smith, *Ethics,* p. 229.

example, in his famous letter to Hutcheson in which he criticizes Butler's view that the moral sense has an authority distinct from its force or strength.[55] But the latter criticism raises issues which will be treated more fully in a later chapter.

CONCLUDING COMMENTS ON HUTCHESON'S THEORY OF MOTIVATION

In his psychological inquiries, Hutcheson, proceeding in the manner of Locke, sets himself the task of describing and reporting the contents of sensation and reflection. To the extent that anyone can report the raw feel of the contents of introspection, Hutcheson does extremely well. He has a considerable talent for discriminating between various kinds of affections and desires and between the more ordinary perceptions of sight, hearing, and touch and what he calls the "finer perceptions" of the sense of beauty and the moral sense. Frankena has observed that, as far as he knows, "Hutcheson is the first British writer to speak of 'simple ideas' in ethics." [56] I might add that, as far as I know, Hutcheson is the first British writer to speak of desire as a "simple idea." "Let it be considered," he says, "that the simple idea of desire is different than that of pain of any kind, or from any sensation whatsoever." [57] As he proceeds with his introspective survey, Hutcheson claims that the term "passion" denotes a "strong, brutal impulse of the will." [58] Pleasure and pain, he claims, are sensations, not passions or affections at all. Hutcheson's theory of motivation seems therefore to offer a classic instance of the sort of empiricist position which has been much attacked by recent writers such as Ryle, Anscombe, Hampshire, and others. They would no doubt complain that he relies heavily upon introspection, that he treats pleasure as a sensation, and that he traces desire and aversion to simple ideas of reflection. Ryle, for example, argues throughout his *Concept of Mind* that desire and pleasure cannot be classified as data of reflection or sensation. And Anscombe joins Ryle in assailing the bad effects resulting from an empiricist epistemology according to which, she claims, not only pleasure but "any sort of wanting would be an internal impression." [59]

Let us take, for example, Hutcheson's doctrine, so much attacked in recent literature, according to which desires are internal events open to

[55] Greig, *The Letters of David Hume*, p. 47.
[56] Frankena, "Hutcheson's Moral Sense Theory," p. 361.
[57] Hutcheson, *Essay*, p. 44.
[58] *Ibid.*, p. 28.
[59] G. E. M. Anscombe, *Intention* (Oxford: Basil Blackwell, 1958), p. 76.

introspection. This view certainly seems open to a large number of objections. Internal events should be localizable, if not exactly in place, at least in time. Desires seem not to be. Furthermore, the concept of desire has logical peculiarities. If desire is a simple idea of reflection, then it should be possible to describe it apart from that object to which it is directed. But, Melden has argued, "that any desire has an object, to use the familiar formula, is a logically necessary and no mere accidental feature of the desire." [60]

Having drawn attention to some of the difficulties which follow from Hutcheson's treatment of desire, we cannot digress into further examination of contemporary discussions of the nature of desire. We might, however, pause to comment briefly on the claim that bad effects follow from Hutcheson's empiricist epistemology and his treatment of pleasure and desire as simple ideas. Granted that he is excessively preoccupied with introspective reports of internal events, his theory of motivation, seen as a whole, nevertheless offers much of worth as regards the explanation of human action. How shall we account for the fact that his practice seems more fortunate than his theory? In doing so, we might make use of a distinction made by R. S. Peters. The latter distinguishes between the use of terms in describing situations and their use in explanations. He maintains that "though terms, like 'pleasure' and 'discomfort' have an important role in *describing* situations, it is doubtful whether they have an explanatory role." [61] What we find, in Hutcheson's case, is that although he does use terms such as "pleasure" and "desire" in describing situations, he also presents explanations in which these terms occur and in which the explanations involve much more than could be gained from his descriptions of internal events. Such explanations appear, for example, in the course of those refutations of psychological egoism and psychological hedonism which show Hutcheson at his best.

Or consider a further example, Hutcheson's distinction between the calm desires and the violent passions. Earlier, it was argued that for Hutcheson, but not for Hume, this is a distinction between two things of different kinds. We even added, parenthetically, that Hutcheson's distinction between calm desires and passions has much in common with Ryle's distinction between inclinations and agitations. But it is important to ask how Hutcheson establishes the existence of a calm desire. Let us take, for example, calm general benevolence. It is surely too much to

---

[60] A. I. Melden, *Free Action* (London: Routledge & Kegan Paul, 1961), p. 109.
[61] R. S. Peters, *The Concept of Motivation* (London: Routledge & Kegan Paul, 1958), p. 140.

suppose that we discover upon introspection an internal event or simple idea having the sort of complex description that would have to attach to calm general benevolence. And the fact is that, apart from his general distinction between the calm and the violent, Hutcheson makes little detailed attempt to trace the characteristics of calm general benevolence to an internal impression.

Having noted the limitations of Hutcheson's appeal to internal events, the question arises as to how his theory might be improved. A thorough answer to this question is beyond the scope of this book. However, a few general comments might be made. Hutcheson is in many respects a radical empiricist in that he makes all sorts of fine discriminations in our experience between what he calls the "finer perceptions" of the sense of beauty and the moral sense, between "calm" or "pure" desires and "violent" passions, and so on. He therefore supposes that we begin with certain internal events having these fantastically complex descriptions and then proceed to formulate explanations of human conduct. But there are philosophical advantages in supposing that the reverse is the case. That is, it is more plausible to suppose that we begin with explanations which may then enter into our descriptions of the internal events in question. For example, instead of attempting to introspect a calm desire, we should then appeal to explanations in the form of principles or rules which concern our long-range goals rather than our impulsive behavior.

But even if the foregoing suggestions concerning deficiencies in Hutcheson's theory are correct, it must be admitted that he still contributes much to our understanding of human motivation. His refutations of egoism and of psychological hedonism, his examination of the place of reason, and his calm desires doctrine remain as notable achievements.

CHAPTER II

HUTCHESON'S MORAL SENSE THEORY

The complete and original title of Hutcheson's *Inquiry* indicates that in this work the principles of Shaftesbury are to be explained and defended against those of Mandeville, the author of the *Fable of the Bees.* There can be no doubt that Hutcheson's moral philosophy owes a great deal to the influence of Anthony Ashley Cooper, the third Earl of Shaftesbury. For this reason I propose to present a very brief examination of some of those issues in Shaftesbury's theory which are related to Hutcheson's moral sense theory.

Discussions of art and morality are to be found throughout all of Shaftesbury's works. However the most sustained analysis of issues concerning morality is to be found in the fourth treatise of his work entitled *Characteristics of Men, Manners, Opinions, Times,* the treatise entitled "An Inquiry Concerning Virtue or Merit." It is to the latter that most of my remarks will be directed.

One of the most notable characteristics of Shaftesbury's theory is his appeal to psychological experience as a foundation for ethics. Other writers had appealed to psychological experience in the development of their ethical theories, but Shaftesbury differs from them in at least two important respects. In the first place, Shaftesbury's account of the psychological bases of ethics differs from that of egoists such a Hobbes. He agrees with Hobbes in seeking a natural basis for morality, but insists that benevolence, justice, beauty and our social impulses are original and not reducible to self-interest. In the second place, Shaftesbury refers to the operation of a reflex sense through which our affections, being reflected upon, give rise to "another kind of affection towards those very affections themselves." [1] In several passages he uses the term "moral sense" and is

---

[1] Anthony Ashley Cooper, Third Earl of Shaftesbury, *Characteristics of Men,*

the first writer to use this term in this context. In making psychological experience central to his account of the bases of morality Shaftesbury differs from authors such as Descartes, Spinoza, Locke, Malebranche, and Cumberland who had often made psychological experience subservient to other principles founded on reason or intuition. Therefore, there is no doubt that Shaftesbury is one of those writers whom Hume had in mind when he referred to those before him who had derived moral distinctions from a moral sense.

But the term "moral sense" and the references to a reflex sense are not as central to Shaftesbury's theory as they are to that of Hutcheson. There can be no doubt that Shaftesbury anticipated Hutcheson's account of the sense of beauty and the moral sense. Again and again he uses such words as "relish" and "taste" in connection with references to the "sense of beauty" and the "sense of right and wrong." However those passages in which Shaftesbury speaks of the sense of beauty and of the moral sense cannot be understood apart from his descriptions of virtue and beauty in terms of the harmony and proportion discoverable in the constitution of human nature.

The view that human nature is a constitution or system is extremely central to Shaftesbury's philosophy and, following him, to the philosophies of Hutcheson and Butler. Although their development of this view has some originality, it was a view which they had certainly encountered in many earlier writers such as Plato and Cicero. Shaftesbury's use of the term "good" follows from his belief that nothing can be called "good" except relatively to the system of which it forms a part.[2] To discover the good for man one must first discover the good of the system or order to which he belongs. But since the good of the parts is discovered only by discovering the good of the system, it is of interest to consider how Shaftesbury describes the largest system of all, the universe. The fact which seems to impress Shaftesbury most about the universe is the presence of order, harmony, and proportion. The harmonies of the universe are compared with those of a work of art. And, just as a work of art presupposes the existence of an artist, so Shaftesbury argues that the harmonies found in the universe reveal the design of a supreme mind. Shaftesbury goes on to assert that such a supreme mind must be entirely good and can have no interest other than the good of the whole. The result is a complete optimism. Whatever is, is right. In a universe in which everything in

Manners, Opinions, Times, ed. by John M. Robertson (2 vols.; New York: Bobbs-Merrill Company, Inc., 1964), I, 251.
    [2] *Ibid.,* I, 243.

nature contributes to an ultimate good, our inability to resolve all discords into harmony and to see the good behind apparent disaster must be ascribed in all cases to our ignorance and limited point of view.

In a universe in which everything contributes to an ultimate good, what is the good for man? Shaftesbury uses the term "good" in several senses which need to be distinguished. He refers at various times to "the good of the system," to "public good," to "self-good" and to "a creature's interest or good." The phrase "good of the system" might conceivably be applied to the ends towards which a universe is directed by a supreme mind. However Shaftesbury generally uses it in connection with the system of rational beings of which each man is a part.[3] Therefore the terms "good of the system" and "public good" become interchangeable. Whenever Shaftesbury uses the term "good" with reference to "public good" or to "self-good" it is clear from the context that the good in question is conceived to be pleasure or satisfaction and that these pleasures or satisfactions constitute happiness. "Self-good" would thus refer to the individual's happiness; "public good," to the happiness of members of the system of rational beings. Furthermore, his view is that in promoting the good of the system of rational beings we are also serving our self-interest.

But what of Shaftesbury's references to a creature's interest or good and to the fact that it is "by affection merely that a creature is esteemed good or ill, *natural* or unnatural?"[4] Here the term "good" has a somewhat different application. Whereas its former use had to do with goodness or value in general, it now is used in connection with actions and the affections from which they spring. Shaftesbury's position may be summarized as follows: An isolated individual might be called "good" if his affections were of such a kind as to bring him satisfaction and enjoyment. However, in opposition to the egoists, Shaftesbury depicts man as a social creature whose nature is such that it shows his relatedness to the system of rational beings of which he forms a part. Good affections are those affections which have regard to the good of the system and a creature is called "good" "when the good or ill of the system to which he has relation is the immediate object of some passion or affection moving him."[5] At the same time, Shaftesbury maintains both that a certain amount of self-regard may be praiseworthy and that some particular benevolent impulses may be blameworthy. What he means is that our particular affections must achieve a balance such that the good of the system will be achieved.

[3] *Ibid.*
[4] *Ibid.,* I, 247.
[5] *Ibid.*

For example, the good of the system may require us both to attend to our health and to restrain an excess of parental concern from interfering with sound judgment as to what is best required for a child's healthy development.

How is such a balance to be achieved? At this stage of the discussion Shaftesbury is speaking of a goodness which may be had not only by man but by sensible creatures in general. Therefore the balance in question, wherever found, is given by nature. It is not the result of choice or conscious reflection. The good affections of a creature exhibit a harmony of which he himself is not aware. The goodness which may be had by all sensible creatures is thus to be contrasted with virtue, which only man can achieve. Shaftesbury maintains that the virtuous man as contrasted with the merely good man must be capable of reflecting on his actions and affections. This reflection gives rise to a new kind of affection. In a famous passage, Shaftesbury describes how actions and affections become the objects of a "reflected sense" so that "by means of this reflected sense, there arises another kind of affection towards those affections themselves, which have been already felt, and are now become the subject of a new liking or dislike." [6] It is important to observe that this new liking or pleasure is, as Shaftesbury says, a "speculative" pleasure. That is, it is not to be confused with those pleasures which consist in the fulfilment of pre-existing desires. For example, a starving man might obtain intense pleasure by satisfying his hunger. If he were to be moved by kindness to share his food with his starving family, his kind act would also bring him pleasure. But if, in addition, he were to reflect on his kind act, he would receive a further pleasure which is to be distinguished from the previous pleasures.

The more one inquires into the intricacies of his theory, the more difficult it becomes to determine exactly what sort of theory Shaftesbury is holding. Take, for example, his claim that the harmonious ordering of the affections is natural and even instinctive. If this harmony of the affections is ascribed to instinct, then the question arises as to whether the existence of a reflex sense is really required in order that we perform right actions. Furthermore, apart from our emotional response to the harmony or balance of affections within man, Shaftesbury is not always clear as to how this harmony itself is to be perceived. He uses such terms as "preconceptions" and "anticipations" [7] which seem to suggest that this harmony may be discerned by intellect. These issues, as we shall see, find

[6] *Ibid.*, I, 251.
[7] *Ibid.*, II, 136.

their way into Hutcheson's philosophy. Therefore we shall attempt to clarify them as they occur in the context of Hutcheson's philosophy rather than in that of Shaftesbury.

However, before turning back to Hutcheson, we might comment briefly on Shaftesbury's treatment of moral judgments. We might suppose that Shaftesbury's emphasis on taste and on amiable feelings would lead him to adopt the view that moral judgments are merely expressive of our feelings. Actually, a study of Shaftesbury's writings indicates that this is not at all the case. It is extremely important to point out that Hume and Hutcheson found in Shaftesbury, not only a theory which describes moral distinctions as originating in a sense, but which at the same time maintains that moral judgments express ways of correcting our sentiments through the adoption of more stable points of view. Such passages as the following need to be kept in mind:

I like! I fancy! I admire! How? By accident, or as I please? No. But I learn to fancy, to admire, to please, as the subjects themselves are deserving, and can bear me out. Otherwise, I like at this hour but dislike the next. I shall be weary of my pursuit, and, upon experience, find little pleasure in the main, if my choice and judgment in it be from no other rule than that single one, because I please.[8]

Passages such as the above lead one to conclude that moral judgments involve an emotional response together with reason and judgment. Commentators seem in agreement, however, that Shaftesbury never succeeded in giving a coherent and plausible account of how these ingredients function together in moral judgments.

THE EPISTEMOLOGICAL BACKGROUND OF HUTCHESON'S MORAL SENSE THEORY

Hutcheson's moral sense doctrine can only be understood in the context of his theory of knowledge. In his theory of knowledge Hutcheson tends to follow and develop the directions laid out by Locke's empiricism and supplemented by Shaftesbury's brief references to the moral sense. The impact of Locke's empiricism upon Hutcheson cannot be overestimated. In spite of some of the curious things that Hutcheson has to say about the moral sense, he nowhere gives up his belief that all simple ideas are gained from sensation and reflection. One of the most striking features of his method is his tendency to appeal to simple and irreducible perceptions, perceptions which other philosophers have overlooked or have attempted

[8] *Ibid.*, I, 218.

to explain away. This appeal is one of the main weapons which he tends to use against both egoists and rationalists. Also, it is this appeal which leads to Hutcheson's surprising discoveries of new senses at the rate of about one every four years!

The term "understanding" is used by Hutcheson as a general term for all of the powers or capacities involved in the attainment of knowledge. Included in these powers are external sensation, consciousness or reflection, judging, reasoning, and, within reflection, those "finer powers of perception," as Hutcheson calls them, of which the most important are the sense of beauty and the moral sense.

The term "sense" is one of the key terms in Hutcheson's philosophy and has special significance for his moral theory because of his claim that moral ideas are derived from a moral sense. The term "sense" always refers to the passive part of the mind. Hutcheson describes a sense as any "determination of our minds to receive ideas independently on our will, and to have perceptions of pleasure and pain." [9]

Let us examine, first of all, the ideas received from the external senses. Hutcheson distinguishes certain perceptions which are "purely sensible" and which, he maintains, are most properly called sensations. There are colors, tastes, smells, sounds, and cold or heat. He suggests that this list may not be complete and that some sensations, such as those of hunger, thirst, weariness, and sickness, are difficult to classify. It is through the external senses that we first receive perceptions of pleasure and pain. Indeed, Hutcheson maintains, "sometimes the sole perception is that of pleasure or pain, as in smells, and the feelings of hunger and thirst." [10] Because of the important place which the concepts of pleasure and pain have in Hutcheson's moral theory, it is worth emphasizing that pleasures and pains are treated as types of sensation and not as types of passion or affection. The pleasures and pains which we receive through the senses are called "natural good" and "natural evil" respectively. Although discussion of the nature of moral goodness must be postponed to a later chapter, confusion may be avoided by remarking that Hutcheson nowhere suggests that natural good is to be identified with moral good.

According to Hutcheson, the sensations which we have been describing, i.e. the secondary qualities and pleasures and pains, are not copies or representations of external objects. However he is concerned to point out their biological role. These sensations are "signals" or "marks" which

---

[9] Hutcheson, *Essay*, p. 4.
[10] *Ibid.*, p. 2.

serve to indicate new events or to indicate "what things are salutory, innocent, or hurtful." [11]

Hutcheson's most interesting observations concerning the primary qualities occur in a brief but extremely provocative footnote contained in the first section of the *Essay*.[12] The primary qualities are not included among the "proper ideas of sensation," i.e. colors, tastes, smells, sounds, and cold or heat, but are said to be "concomitant ideas" or ideas which accompany our sensations. For example, ideas of number and duration may accompany, not only our external sensations, but also our ideas gained from reflection. Other ideas of extension, figure, motion, and rest may accompany the most different sensations. Strictly speaking, Hutcheson's account of the primary qualities cannot be reconciled with his view that all of our ideas are gained from sensation and reflection. The primary qualities can be said to be gained from sensation only in the sense that they accompany sensations. He regards primary qualities and the external world as being established by God through laws of nature.

The external senses having been examined, let us turn to a consideration of the nature of reflection. Because Hutcheson's use of terms tends to be somewhat confusing, it is necessary to begin by clarifying what is meant by the terms "consciousness," "reflection," "internal sense," and "reflex sense." The terms "reflection," "consciousness," and "internal sense" are used by Hutcheson as synonyms. These terms denote the capacities by which the modifications of the mind, i.e. perceptions ,judgments, reasonings, affections, and feelings, are known as objects. This is the language and terminology of Locke's *Essay*. Locke was by no means the only writer to have described such a process of reflection. However, many philosophers, influenced by the traditions of scholastic philosophy, described reflection as an intellectual operation. For example, Spinoza's doctrine of the "idea ideae" has reference to a type of reflection which is intellectual. H. A. Wolfson states that "this *idea ideae* in the sense of both consciousness and rational knowledge is also described in Spinoza by the terms 'reflective knowledge' (*cognitio reflexiva*) and 'reflective idea' (*idea reflexiva*), terms which are of scholastic origin." [13] Hutcheson, following Locke, presents an account of reflection as a sort of "internal sense" which is "reflexive" in that it turns inward upon our mental states. As such it is not to be thought of merely as a process of thinking or meditating about our previous experiences.

[11] Hutcheson, *System*, p. 5.
[12] Hutcheson, *Essay*, p. 3n.
[13] Wolfson, *The Philosophy of Spinoza*, II, 94.

But if "reflection" is described as "reflexive" how is the term "reflection" to be distinguished from the term "reflex sense"? According to Hutcheson, reflection is itself a sort of "internal sensation" by means of which the mind takes note of its states. But, in addition, the perceptions of both sensation and reflection may be antecedent to new perceptions of the so-called "reflex senses." The classic source of this doctrine is the following passage from Shaftesbury:

In a creature capable of forming general notions of things, not only the outward beings which offer themselves to the sense are objects of the affection but the very actions themselves, and the affections of pity, kindness, gratitude, and their contraries, being brought into the mind by reflection, become objects. So that, by means of this reflected sense, there arises another kind of affection towards those very affections themselves, which have been already felt, and are now become the subject of a new liking or dislike.[14]

Shaftesbury refers to this "reflected sense" as the moral sense, although it is of interest to note that the latter term is used by him only a few times and even then usually only in his marginal notes. If it this doctrine of a "reflected sense" which Hutcheson proceeds to develop in connection with the sense of beauty and the moral sense, and, furthermore, in connection with his discoveries of other senses such as the "public sense" and the "sense of honor."

THE NATURE AND FUNCTION OF THE MORAL SENSE

Let us now consider more closely the nature and function of the moral sense as described by Hutcheson. In this chapter my comments will be restricted, for the most part, to Hutcheson's moral sense doctrine as found in those earlier works which were of greatest historical significance, namely, the *Inquiry*, the *Essay*, and the *Illustrations*. In these works, there is one version of the moral sense doctrine which is given an overwhelming emphasis by Hutcheson. The outlines of this version may be indicated rather briefly. In the preface to his *Inquiry Concerning Beauty, Order, Harmony and Design*, Hutcheson is preoccupied with some of the pleasures of the imagination which had been discussed in one of Joseph Addison's essays in the *Spectator* [15] and by Shaftesbury. Hutcheson is especially concerned with two kinds of pleasure, namely, those which

---

[14] Shaftesbury, *Characteristics*, I, 251.
[15] *The Spectator*, ed. by Henry Morley (3 vols.; London: George Routledge and Sons, Limited, 1891), II, 714.

arise following our contemplation of order and regularity and those which arise when we contemplate acts of a certain kind. The first of these he ascribes to a sense of beauty, the second, to a moral sense. As regards the moral sense, he is concerned to emphasize not only that it is a source of unique pleasures and pains but also that, contrary to the egoists, these pleasures and pains are not traceable to self-love. Of the moral sense, he says: "we mean by it only a determination of our minds to receive amiable or disagreeable ideas of actions, when they occur to our observation, antecedent to any opinions of advantage or loss to redound to our selves for them. . . ." [16]

In Hutcheson's revisions of his earliest formulation of the moral sense theory, a very important change occurs in that there is much greater emphasis on the term "approval." The above quotation from the second edition, dated 1726, refers to a determination to receive "amiable or disagreable ideas of actions." In the third and later editions this becomes "a determination of our minds to receive the simple ideas of approbation or condemnation." From the context, however, it is not to be doubted that, no matter how unique they may be, approval and disapproval are still kinds of pleasure and pain.

Although Hutcheson, in the works we have been considering, places great emphasis on the moral sense as simply a source of unique pleasures and pains, there are numerous phrases which are very difficult to render consistent with this doctrine. What are we to make of references to "perceptions of moral excellence" and to moral goodness as a "quality apprehended in actions which procures approbation"? [17]

Some of the perplexities arising from these expressions may be removed by examining the question whether Hutcheson's moral sense is to be regarded as a source of sensations or of feelings. The answer to this question is best discovered by careful attention to the terminology and character of Hutcheson's theory of knowledge as outlined earlier in this chapter. Hutcheson says of approval and condemnation that these are probably simple ideas which cannot be further explained, or "which can only be explained by synonymous words, or by concomitant or consequent circumstances." [18] Like any other simple ideas, these must be attributed to some sense or other. Notice that internal powers of perception are all called "senses." This is the language of Locke who wrote of reflection that "this source of *ideas* every man has wholly in himself; and though it be

---

[16] Selby-Bigge, *British Moralists*, I, 84.
[17] *Ibid.*, I, 69.
[18] Hutcheson, *Illustrations*, p. 208.

not sense, as having nothing to do with external objects, yet it is very like it, and might properly enough be called internal sense." [19] However, Locke does not stress the use of the term "internal sensation" from which one may gather that he might agree with Gibson who contends that "there are essential respects in which [Locke's] view of the nature and function of reflection differs even from his own conception of sensation." [20]

In this context Hutcheson develops a somewhat curious terminology. He lays more stress than Locke does on the term "internal sensation" as a synonym for reflection. And of course the terms "reflex sense," "moral sense," and "internal sense" are also taken over from Shaftesbury. This terminology is the more curious in that Hutcheson is if anything less disposed than Locke towards exploring any literal interpretation of a strict likeness between reflection and sensation. For one thing, he is less inclined to representationalism than Locke, i.e. to the doctrine that our ideas represent an existence in an external world. Even Locke had not pursued his representationalism as regards reflection. Aaron makes the following statement:

As we follow Locke in his account of these operations of the mind, perception, memory, comparison, and so on, the representationalism is not at all apparent. . . . There is no hesitation in accepting the evidence of reflection on its face value.[21]

These remarks may also be applied to Hutcheson. His references to all sorts of senses as extensions of Locke's doctrine of reflection is neither to be taken as implying a narrow and strict analogy with sensation nor as suggesting that such senses acquaint us with some objective quality or characteristic.

The foregoing remarks give us some indication as to how a number of Hutcheson's curious phrases are to be interpreted. To perceive moral excellence or moral goodness is to experience a certain kind of pleasure and, from the way that the term "approval" is substituted for the term "pleasure," we may gather that to feel approval is to feel pleasure of a certain kind. A very important fact concerning this sort of terminology is that Hutcheson never identifies these perceptions with "passions." That we feel approval is not a complete reason for doing. However, our feeling of approval may give rise to a desire which *is* a complete reason for doing.

If the foregoing description of Hutcheson's terminology is correct, it is impossible to ascribe to him what Broad calls "the naively realistic form

[19] Locke, *Essay*, I, 78.
[20] James Gibson, *Locke's Theory of Knowledge and Its Historical Relations* (Cambridge, Eng.: Cambridge University Press, 1960), p. 56.
[21] Richard I. Aaron, *John Locke* (2d ed.; Oxford: Clarendon Press, 1955), p. 130.

of the moral sense theory." [22] According to this form of the moral sense theory, Hutcheson's treatment of approval would be interpreted as analogous to the way in which visual sensation is described by the naively realistic view of visual perception. The moral sense would be a capacity for cognizing the virtue or moral goodness of actions or character-dispositions and these moral characteristics would be held to be simple empirical qualities. Anyone who has considered Hutcheson's epistemology and his early treatment of the moral sense as a source of pleasure cannot fail to consider this an utterly implausible interpretation of Hutcheson's theory, taken as a whole. Nowhere does his epistemology suggest a naively realistic theory of sensation and, more important, his "internal sense" and "moral sense" are even less conformable to this theory. To adopt Aaron's statement concerning Locke which I quoted earlier, Hutcheson may be said to accept both the evidence of reflection in general and the moral sense in particular at "face value." That is, no representationalist or naively realistic interpretation can be made of his statements concerning the perceptions gained from these sources.

Let us pause to pull together some of the foregoing comments. In the course of outlining the main directions of Hutcheson's moral sense theory, we encountered a number of phrases which were difficult to interpret. Among these were his references to perceptions of moral excellence and to moral goodness as a quality which we apprehend. An examination of Hutcheson's epistemology in general and of his conception of the moral sense in particular led us to conclude that a naively realistic interpretation is, generally speaking, foreign to his outlook. We suggested, therefore, that in most of the passages in which Hutcheson refers to perceptions of moral excellence or to apprehending moral goodness, we may gather from the context that to perceive moral excellence or to apprehend moral goodness is simply to feel approbation.

In spite of the fact that we are thereby able to interpret most of the troublesome passages to which we have referred, some passages remain which, although small in number, are an embarrassment to an interpretation aiming at consistency. These remaining passages tend to have in common a naively realistic terminology and the apparent claim that moral goodness is an objective quality which is somehow apprehended. Passages in which the moral sense is referred to as a faculty and in which moral excellence is referred to as an independent quality are to be found mostly in the *System*. In a later chapter we shall raise questions concerning the extent to which the latter references constitute changes from

---

[22] Broad, "Moral-Sense Theories in Ethics," p. 371.

Hutcheson's earlier position. But there are other difficult passages of the sort in question which are sprinkled throughout his earlier works. Indeed, the very opening of the *Inquiry* confronts us with the statement that moral goodness is a "quality apprehended in actions which procures approbation." [23]

Let us consider two interpretations of Hutcheson which seek to explain the remaining difficult passages we have been considering. The first is that of James Ward Smith; the second, that of William K. Frankena.

In brief, what James Ward Smith maintains is that, as he puts it, "however much Hutcheson stresses the motive character of our moral approval, our moral judgments do not indicate that approval." [24] What then do they indicate? Smith attributes to Shaftesbury and Hutcheson the view that in addition to a feeling of approval all valuational situations have in common an additional feature, namely, "the tendency of all x's to lead to harmony or social welfare." [25] According to Smith, it is this feature which is indicated.

We may now reflect briefly on those characteristics of Hutcheson's position which lend support to Smith's interpretation. There seems to be little doubt that Hutcheson shared Shaftesbury's conviction that nature in general and human nature in particular exhibit a constitution or order. Shaftesbury maintained that this constitution is approved by the moral sense and is a source of pleasure to the sense of beauty. These elements find their way into Hutcheson's philosophy. When the objection is raised that, after all, the approval of the moral sense is arbitrary, he falls back on the argument that God, too, has a moral sense not unlike ours. This was the sort of theory, held by Shaftesbury and Hutcheson, which Hume criticized as involving an appeal to final causes.

We referred earlier to the fact that Shaftesbury provides no clear description of how the harmony of affections within man is to be perceived. His use of such terms as "pre-conceptions" and "anticipations" does not clarify whether or not the constitution in question is discerned by intellect and certainly does not show unambiguously that this is the work of a moral sense. These difficulties are transferred to Hutcheson's theory whenever he returns to the doctrine of a "constitution" and its relation to the moral sense.

It may be added that Hutcheson was no doubt influenced also by the emphasis on the concept of a "constitution" in Butler's philosophy. But

---

[23] Selby-Bigge, *British Moralists*, I, 69.
[24] James Ward Smith, "The British Moralists and the Fallacy of Psychologism," *Journal of the History of Ideas,* XI, No. 2 (1950), 165.
[25] *Ibid.,* p. 175.

here again Hutcheson received little help in the formulation of an exact theory as to how ethical characteristics and this "constitution" are known. Butler contributes rather little to the reason versus moral sense controversy, declaring at one point, the following:

It is manifest great part of common language, and of common behavior over the world, is formed upon supposition of such a moral faculty, whether called conscience, moral reason, moral sense or divine reason; whether considered as a sentiment of the understanding or as a perception of the heart, or, which seems the truth, as including both.[26]

How might Hutcheson have assimilated these doctrines which he found in Shaftesbury and Butler into a consistent theory? Let us suppose, for a moment, that he did adopt the sort of view ascribed to him by James Ward Smith to the effect that approval is present in all valuational situations but is not to be identified with moral goodness, which is an objective quality. His adoption of this sort of view would account for the naively realistic language in which he speaks of apprehending moral goodness. Furthermore, his adoption of this sort of view is strongly suggested by passages in the *System* such as the following:

When we admire the virtue of another, the whole excellence, or that quality which by nature we are determined to approve, is conceived to be in that other; we are pleased in the contemplation because the object is excellent and the object is not judged to be therefore excellent because it gives us pleasure.[27]

Frankena's interpretation is concerned for the most part with Hutcheson's earlier theory. Frankena tries very hard to interpret the naively realistic terminology in such a manner as to make it consistent with his view that the moral sense is not cognitive at all. He suggests that in some of the troublesome passages in question "apprehended" might mean "judged to be" and that the phrase "perceiving moral excellence" need not imply a naively realistic interpretation.[28] Plausible as his suggestions are in some cases, there are many in which his interpretation is strained. Take, for example, the very opening sentence of the *Inquiry*: "The word moral goodness, in this *Treatise,* denotes our idea of some quality apprehended in actions, which procures approbation." [29] The very terms "quality" and "apprehended," separated as they are from the term

[26] Joseph Butler, *Dissertation II: Of The Nature of Virtue* in Selby-Bigge, *British Moralists,* I, 246.
[27] Hutcheson, *System,* p. 54.
[28] Frankena, "Hutcheson's Moral Sense Theory," p. 369.
[29] Selby-Bigge, *British Moralists,* I, 69.

"approbation," lend themselves far more readily to a naively realistic interpretation.

Let us try to take a synoptic view of the issues under consideration. We considered earlier the main outlines of Hutcheson's moral sense theory and came to the conclusion that in using the term "moral sense" he does not intend to imply a strict analogy with sensation, nor does he intend a naively realistic point of view. However, is seems that Hutcheson was inconsistent and that he did at times fall back on the sort of theory ascribed to him by James Ward Smith. Although this sort of theory is more evident in his later works, I have also referred to passages in the *Inquiry* and *Essay* in which it occurs. But it is one thing to find certain passages in Hutcheson which retain elements of Shaftesbury's theory and which combine this with naively realistic terminology. It is quite another to give undue prominence to these passages and to interpret his entire ethical theory in terms of them. This is what has been done by commentators such as James Martineau [30] and James Ward Smith. Martineau tends to overemphasize the theory which he claims to find in the *System,* with its numerous references to the "moral faculty" and to "moral excellence" as a quality in actions. James Ward Smith also seems to overemphasize those passages throughout Hutcheson's work which might be taken to refer to objective moral characteristics which the moral sense approves. These passages run counter to others which, we have claimed, figure much more prominently in Hutcheson's theory. By contrast, Frankena attempts to interpret Hutcheson in such a way as to make the latter hold consistently to the view that the moral sense is not cognitive at all. But, we have claimed, such an attempt is only partially successful in view of the fact that there are passages occurring throughout Hutcheson's theory which resist the sort of treatment Frankena prescribes.

Hutcheson must therefore be said to have failed to assimilate and render consistent some of the doctrines which he took over from Shaftesbury. The naively realistic side of his theory, according to which the moral sense would cognize some empirical characteristic, remains undeveloped. Worse still, a naively realistic terminology in his moral sense doctrine conflicts with the fact that a naively realistic theory is entirely foreign to his general epistemological position.

---

[30] James Martineau, *Types of Ethical Theory* (2 vols.; 3d ed., rev.; Oxford: Clarendon Press, 1891), II, 537.

Let us now turn to Hutcheson's theory concerning the analysis, nature, and function of moral judgments. In doing so, it is rather evident that although he has much to say on this topic and although much more is implicit in what he says, he does not address himself to this topic in the manner of a contemporary writer. He lacks our terminology and has not made distinctions which have long been familiar to us. Sometimes he dismisses rather contemptuously issues concerning moral language. At other times he is extremely painstaking concerning these issues as, for example, in his treatment of how our sentiments are "corrected" in the expression of moral judgments. Pall S. Ardal has written of Hume as follows:

> Hume does not give us, in the *Treatise,* a theory of moral language, but an account of the nature and origin of evaluations. If Ethics is defined as the analysis of moral discourse, Hume's *Treatise* does not contain much in the way of Ethics. What it does contain is an account of the way the concepts of virtue and vice have their source in human emotions.[31]

This sort of comment, I submit, is too strong as applied to either Hutcheson or Hume. Concentrating on Hutcheson, it is extremely important to emphasize that he does not provide an adequate and complete theory of moral language. However it is only fair to note that he does give important indications of such a theory. He distinguishes between "natural good" and "moral good," between "interested obligation" and what we should call "moral obligation," between "exciting reasons" and "justifying reasons," and contributes significantly to the discussion of how our moral judgments correct our sentiments. Furthermore, considering the interest in his theory, it seems not at all inappropriate to speculate on the type of theory which he held or even which he would have held had he employed some of our terminology.

In attempting to discover what sort of theory Hutcheson holds, it is helpful to employ some of the terms used by Broad in his exhaustive article dealing with the moral sense theories, terms which are for the most part employed also by Frankena in his important article on Hutcheson. Let us distinguish, then, the following positions which are relevant, in one way or another, to a discussion of Hutcheson's theory: (1) The Naively Realistic form of the Moral Sense Theory; (2) The Subjective form of the

---

[31] Pall S. Ardal, *Passion and Value in Hume's Treatise* (Edinburgh: Edinburgh University Press, 1966), p. 212.

Moral Sense Theory; (3) The Non-cognitive forms of the Moral Sense Theory. I use the latter heading rather than the term "Interjectional" used by Broad and Frankena for two reasons. In the first place, the term "Interjectional Theory" suggests the assimilation of ethical sentences to interjections, a view which has had little acceptance. In the second place, I shall distinguish Non-cognitive forms of the Moral Sense Theory which cannot be equated with Frankena's description of the Interjectional Theory as a theory which "regards ethical utterances as purely emotive, expressively or dynamically – as expressing and evoking emotions." [32]

Let us begin with the Naively Realistic form of the Moral Sense Theory. This is the only one of the theories to be considered which lays any stress on the term "sense." After all, the term "moral sense" suggests analogies with sense perception. Those who hold a naively realistic theory of sense perception would maintain that the judgment "X is red" is made when our sense of sight reveals to us an objective quality of redness which exists just as we perceive it. A naively realistic form of the moral sense theory would maintain, correspondingly, that we have a moral sense which reveals to us an objective quality which exists independently and just as we perceive it. On this theory ethical judgments are cognitive. Hutcheson's arguments against the rationalists are intended to prove, among other things, that the ethical characteristic revealed to our moral sense is empirical.

While discussing the nature of the moral sense in the foregoing sections of this chapter, we considered a number of comments and arguments which bear on the Naively Realistic form of the Moral Sense Theory. Reviewed briefly, they are as follows. Hutcheson's general epistemological position is not naively realistic. His treatment of sensation nowhere suggests a naively realistic interpretation. And reasons were given for maintaining that his doctrine of reflection does not lend itself to naively realistic or representationalistic interpretations. Broad's exposition of the Naively Realistic form of the Moral Sense Theory develops the analogy with sensation. But, it should be insisted, the moral sense is an "internal sense"; it is on the side of reflection, not sensation. This being the case, it is completely foreign to Hutcheson's outlook to force a naively realistic interpretation on the perceptions of the moral sense.

To account for Hutcheson's naively realistic sounding terminology I maintained that there are a few passages in Hutcheson's early theory and considerably more in his later works which suggest a position, reminiscent of Shaftesbury and sometimes of Butler, according to which ethical char-

[32] Frankena, "Hutcheson's Moral Sense Theory," p. 366.

acteristics are objective and are not to be identified with feelings of approval. But, as I pointed out, this position, undoubtedly present, is never developed consistently. I shall maintain, later in this book, that some of Hutcheson's later references to such a position grow out of his awareness of serious difficulties in his earlier account of the moral sense.

Next to be considered is the Subjective form of the Moral Sense Theory. According to this view, moral judgments are cognitive and refer to certain sensations, emotions, or feelings experienced by human beings. This is a form of naturalism according to which ethical characteristics are reducible to or definable in terms of empirical characteristics without remainder. Further divisions within the theory in question occur depending on whether the sensations, emotions, or feelings referred to are those of the speaker, of most people, or of people who fulfil certain qualifications, notably those qualifications which would be ascribed to a so-called "ideal observer."

The first variety of the Subjective Theory to be considered is that which maintains that moral judgments refer to the sensations, emotions or feelings of the speaker. These references might be further classified as directed either to occurrent experiences or to dispositions. It is in trying to discover what Hutcheson's view would be regarding such a theory that one comes to the conclusion that he has neglected woefully many problems pertaining to the nature of ethical discourse. Certain observations come to mind in this connection relating not only to the theory in question, but to all theories which might be attributed to him. There is a good deal of evidence, much of which has been already presented, which would lead one to suppose that, on Hutcheson's theory, when one utters a moral judgment there are two elements present, namely, a feeling of approval, occurrent or dispositional, and certain characteristics giving rise to that approval. The question then arises as to the relationship between moral goodness and approval. Should we, in Broad's terms, give a "phenomenalist" or "causal" analysis of the expression "X is morally good"? A "causal analysis" would take the form of maintaining that moral goodness is the property that *causes* an act to be approved. A "phenomenalist analysis," according to Broad, "would be that goodness is the characteristic of *being* generally approved by men." [33] But, we might add, the approval might also be held to be that of the speaker or of a group having certain qualifications. Hume is full of passages suggesting some sort of "phenomenalist analysis." Take, for example, the following: "We do not

[33] C. D. Broad, *Five Types of Ethical Theory* (London: Routledge & Kegan Paul Ltd., 1930), p. 109.

infer a character to be virtuous, because it pleases: But in feeling that it pleases after such a particular manner, we in effect feel that it is virtuous." [34] Hutcheson, although he would often seem to agree, seldom states explicitly this sort of view. However, our previous examination of his theory leads us to suppose that he would be, at least in his early theory, a fervent supporter of the "phenomenalist analysis."

Yet when he comes to define "moral goodness" Hutcheson is often equivocal. Consider, for example, the following which he includes in a list of what he calls "definitions": "An action is morally good, when it flows from benevolent affection, or intention of absolute good to others." [35] In the light of his moral sense doctrine this would seem best interpreted as proferring, not a definition of "moral goodness," but a statement *about* "moral goodness," and about the characteristic which evokes in us that approval which he elsewhere seems to identify with moral goodness. Regrettably, Hutcheson fails to make a needed distinction between definitions of ethical terms and statements about those characteristics in virtue of which we say that an act has an ethical characteristic such as "moral goodness" or "obligatoriness."

Although his earlier theory strongly suggests that he would favor a "phenomenalist analysis" of "X is morally good," one of the few passages in which he is unequivocal occurs in a later work, the *System*. We find there the following statement which clearly indicates his support of a "causal analysis" in which virtue is a quality, independent of pleasure or approval, which causes pleasure or approval in us.

When we admire the virtue of another, the whole excellence, or that quality which by nature we are determined to approve, is conceived to be in that other; we are pleased in the contemplation because the object is excellent and the object is not judged to be therefore excellent because it gives us pleasure.[36]

This sort of passage simply cannot be rendered consistent with his earlier views and suggests the presence of a different sort of theory in the *System*.

We have been considering some of the problems which arise when one tries to discover whether or not Hutcheson holds that variety of the Subjective Theory according to which moral judgments refer to the sensations, emotions, or feelings of the speaker. He nowhere presents an unequivocal statement of this extremely implausible view. The best evidence that he definitely does not hold it comes from those passages which tend to sup-

[34] Hume, *Treatise,* p. 471.
[35] Hutcheson, *Essay,* p. 38.
[36] Hutcheson, *System,* p. 54.

port the trans-subjective, dispositional form of the Subjective Theory, to which we shall now turn.

The form of the moral sense theory next to be considered is again a Subjective Theory which holds in this case that moral judgments such as "X is obligatory" or "X is morally good" may be analyzed in terms of the statement "X would be approved by anyone who might contemplate it." Or, instead of appealing to just anyone, qualifications may be added to characterize the so-called "ideal spectator." These qualifications might include impartiality, being fully informed, being in a normal frame of mind, and perhaps even others. This is again a form of naturalism according to which ethical statements are cognitive. This type of theory is stated above in its dispositional form. Because reference is to dispositions rather than to occurrent emotions, this theory brings out the fact that moral judgments may have a corrective role in altering and restraining our variable sentiments.

Let us consider, therefore, whether Hutcheson did in fact hold this theory and in what form. There are a great number of passages which tend to support Broad's contention that holders of the moral sense doctrine defended this position in its trans-subjective and dispositional form. The most famous of these passages is no doubt the following: "When we say one is obliged to an action, we mean . . . that every spectator, or he himself upon reflection, must approve his action, and disapprove his omitting it, if he considers fully all its circumstances." [37]

To hold the Subjective Theory in its trans-subjective and dispositional form is to hold a type of naturalism. Now this in itself may provoke the objection that ethical statements are simply not reducible without remainder to statements about some non-ethical characteristics such as feelings of approval. But leaving aside this general objection for the moment, let us look more closely at the theory held by Hutcheson. It seems evident that he is not arguing for a statistical appeal to what most human beings do in fact approve. Instead, his theory is classifiable as a type of what Broad calls "Ideal" as opposed to "Factual" Naturalism.[38] By its reference to dispositions and ideal attitudes rather than occurrent feelings, Ideal Naturalism allows for the corrective function of moral judgments.

This appeal to Ideal Naturalism is attended with certain difficulties which must now be considered, namely, (1) the problem of moral disagreement and (2) the tendency for ethical characteristics to infiltrate into

[37] Hutcheson, *Illustrations*, p. 232.
[38] Broad, *Five Types of Ethical Theory*, p. 262.

one's description of the ideal spectator. Let us see whether or not these difficulties arise in Hutcheson's theory. It was claimed above that Hutcheson is not arguing for a statistical survey of what most human beings do in fact approve. But neither does he appear to be arguing for a statistical survey of what would be approved by ideal spectators. He seems, as in his definition of "obligation" quoted earlier, to equate the ideal spectator with what the speaker himself would approve upon reflection. His method seems to suggest that to discover what an ideal spectator would approve we look inward, trying to find ourselves in that normal, impartial, and informed frame of mind in which the peculiarly moral attitude which he refers to as "approval" will emerge. If his theory does direct us outward to a study of the responses of ideal spectators, the objection is raised as to whether such ideal spectators can be found, and if found, whether they would exhibit moral agreement. If, on the other hand, his theory directs us inward, similar difficulties occur as we wonder whether we are fully reflective, informed, impartial etc., and whether, even if we are, our approval will always be constant.

We must conclude that, like other exponents of Ideal Naturalism, Hutcheson has problems with moral disagreement. He seems to be less inclined towards the other source of difficulty, the tendency for ethical characteristics to infiltrate into the ideal characteristics of the spectator. For example, Hutcheson never suggests that the ideal spectator must also be "benevolent" or "moral."

But we have left until the last a final group of objections to the trans-subjective, dispositional form of the Subjective Theory. These have to do with the relationships existing between ethical characteristics and certain non-ethical characteristics upon which the ethical characteristics seem to be grounded. Broad summarizes these objections to the trans-subjective, dispositional form of the Subjective Theory as follows:

(i) Can it deal with the fact that judgments like "That act is right" seem always to be grounded upon the presence in the act of some non-ethical right-inclining characteristic, such as being the fulfilment of a promise? (ii) If so, can it deal with the further fact that the connexion between a right-inclining characteristic and the rightness which it tends to convey seems to be necessary and synthetic? And (iii) can it deal with the fact that it seems not only intelligible but also true to say that the moral pro-emotion is felt towards an act in respect of the characteristic of *rightness* and moral anti-emotion in respect of the characteristic of wrongness? [39]

These are extremely serious objections to the theory in question. But because they arise again in connection with certain types of non-cognitive

[39] Broad, "Moral-Sense Theories in Ethics," p. 376.

theory about to be considered, I shall avoid repetition by postponing further comment concerning them.

In his influential article entitled "Hutcheson's Moral Sense Theory," William K. Frankena has argued that Hutcheson is an early exponent of the non-cognitivist theory. Frankena claims that Hutcheson, like other non-cognitivists, is maintaining that moral judgments are expressive of emotional reactions and that since these judgments are not statements of any kind whatsoever they are neither true nor false. As distinguished from some non-cognitivists, Hutcheson maintains that the sort of reaction expressed is a unique sort of pleasure or what might be called a "peculiarly moral attitude." Frankena ascribes to Hutcheson a further view which, he claims, is distinctive of the latter's version of non-cognitivism, namely, the view that moral judgments are based on what Hutcheson calls "justifying reasons."

Let us examine some of Frankena's reasons for believing that Hutcheson did not hold a Subjective Theory. Frankena admits that there are no explicit statements which rule out a subjectivist reading of Hutcheson, but suggests that certain features of Hutcheson's position do imply that such a reading is untenable. The first of these is the fact that Hutcheson does not seem to be conducting the sort of statistical study of actual or possible feelings of approval that would be required by the Subjective Theory. Instead, Frankena claims, Hutcheson depicts the moral sense as reacting to contemplated actions with approval or disapproval.[40]

One can imagine a wily exponent of the Subjective Theory answering that to feel approbation is not to be identified with uttering a moral judgment. Moral judgments might still be trans-subjective and dispositional. However Frankena is right in pointing out that the Subjective Theorist is then committed to a statistical investigation of actual or possible feelings of approval. As it was pointed out earlier, Hutcheson seems to suggest that to discover what an ideal spectator would approve we look inward and try to discover what we would approve upon reflection. This method, together with the assumption which too readily accompanies it that all men will agree in their attitudes, fails to take sufficient account of the problems concerning moral disagreement. That this method is not strictly that of the trans-subjective and dispositional form of the Subjective Theory does indeed, as Frankena correctly argues, "establish a presumption that he does not hold this theory." [41]

[40] Frankena, "Hutcheson's Moral Sense Theory," p. 371.
[41] Ibid.

Frankena goes on to a further argument which is intended to prove that Hutcheson cannot hold a Subjective Theory of any kind whatsoever. He puts it as follows:

A strict subjective theory would seem to be inconsistent with at least the spirit of what Hutcheson is contending when he says that moral distinctions are not perceived by reason but by a sense. For on a subjective view moral judgments are empirical propositions about the incidence of pleasure and pain, etc., and so are subject to empirical investigation. But then they are deliverances, not of some sense, but of our power of discovering true propositions, which, by Hutcheson's definition, is reason.[42]

I believe that this argument can be shown to be unsound. The issue concerns the meaning of the term "empirical proposition." According to Hutcheson's theory of knowledge, a proposition may both be of the sort that we should today call empirical and at the same time be a proposition whose truth is discoverable by reason. Let us try to clarify this somewhat confusing position. Hutcheson is in these respects, as in so many others, following Locke. Like Locke, Hutcheson maintains as firmly as any empiricist that sensation and reflection provide the ultimate materials of knowledge. But they do not provide knowledge itself. In Book IV of his *Essay,* Locke gives a "rationalistic" or even "intuitionistic" account of the manner in which the materials given in sensation and reflection are related in the mind.[43] For Locke and Hutcheson, knowledge consists of the intuition of a relation between ideas given in experience. Thus, it would be quite possible for Hutcheson to maintain a Subjective Theory, for, in that case, even though it is reason that discovers the truth of propositions, these propositions might well relate elements given by our moral sense. It may be remarked, as most commentators seem to agree, that the wedding of these intuitionist and empiricistic elements in Locke's theory of knowledge is not very successful.

At this point we are left with the conclusion that, contrary to Frankena, Hutcheson is not prevented from holding a Subjective Theory by his analysis of the functions of reason and of the moral sense. We have agreed, however, with Frankena's claim that a presumption is established that Hutcheson is not maintaining a Subjective Theory. It must surely be insisted that this presumption is somewhat slight. Because Hutcheson devotes so little attention to the study of moral discourse, one hesitates to attribute to him any clear appreciation of the distinctions made current

---

[42] *Ibid.*
[43] The relations between Locke's intuitionism and empiricism are discussed by Richard I. Aaron in his *John Locke,* p. 224.

by the disputes between cognitivists and non-cognitivists. Leaving aside the question of Hutcheson's own intentions, it seems to me that his theory is slightly more consistent with some form of non-cognitivism than with a cognitive Subjective Theory. And because of the fact that Hutcheson as a naturalist would be subject to the familiar charges that have left naturalism refuted in the minds of most commentators, it is perhaps the more interesting to examine whether or not his theory is more viable if given a non-cognitivist reading.

We must therefore inquire more closely into the sort of non-cognitivist theory which might be ascribed to Hutcheson. As described earlier, Frankena's interpretation attributes to Hutcheson's theory two characteristics which are not shared by all non-cognitivist theories: (1) the attitude expressed in moral judgments is a unique sort of pleasure and might be referred to as a "peculiarly moral attitude"; (2) moral judgments expressing this attitude are based on what Hutcheson calls "justifying reasons."

Let us postpone comment on the first of the above characteristics of Hutcheson's theory and consider instead the second, which concerns the conception of moral reasoning implied by Hutcheson's account of the nature and function of justifying reasons. The sort of non-cognitive theory which we have been ascribing to Hutcheson might take one of two possible forms as regards the nature of moral reasoning. According to the first, the relationship between reasons and moral judgments is causal. According to the second, this relationship is in some sense logical.

The first of these forms of non-cognitive theory has been defended by Stevenson. According to Stevenson, evaluative utterances are expressive of approval and the reasons which are relevant to them are reasons for approving. He argues as follows concerning the relationship between reasons and ethical judgments:

> Suppose that a theorist should *tabulate* the "valid" inferences from R's [reasons] to E's [ethical judgments]. It is difficult to see how he could be doing anything more than specify what R's he thereby resolves to *accept* as supporting the various E's. . . . Under the name of "validity" he will be selecting those inferences to which he is psychologically disposed to give assent, and perhaps inducing others to give a similar assent to them.[44]

There is, however, a different account of moral reasoning which might be defended by a non-cognitivist. Indeed many cognitivists and non-cognitivists alike have argued that reasons for approving are not simply

[44] Charles L. Stevenson, *Ethics and Language* (New Haven: Yale University Press, 1944), p. 171.

causes for approving. Instead such reasons serve to indicate that something or other is worthy of approval. According to this sort of view, moral reasoning, although unlike deductive or inductive reasoning, nevertheless serves to validate moral judgments and not merely to provide complex causal explanations of their occurrence. Ideally, moral reasoning exhibits a set of principles which would govern our moral deliberation and justification and would be intersubjectively valid.

What sort of theory of moral reasoning does Hutcheson hold? Since his theory is far from straightforward, the answer to this question must be rather complex. Some of the characteristics of his theory can best be exhibited by considering some aspects of Frankena's interpretation of it. Frankena gives the following summary of Hutcheson's position:

For Hutcheson justifying reasons ultimately consist of propositions about the benevolent or malevolent motives and results of actions or characters. Why is A or his action morally good? Ultimately because it promotes or is intended to promote the general welfare. Why ought B to do so and so? Ultimately because this is for the greatest good. But why should we do what is for the general good? On Hutcheson's view this is the end of the line as far as justifying reasons go. . . . A final justifying reason simply is a proposition to which the moral sense reacts favorably as such.[45]

This seems to me an accurate description of Hutcheson's position. Now according to this view it would seem that there need be no logical connection between the reaction of the moral sense and justifying reasons. There would be no inconsistency in supposing that someone might acknowledge the presence of a certain fact, e.g. that an act is benevolent, and yet at the same time might react with disapproval or indeed might not react at all. In these respects, Hutcheson's view of moral reasoning is consistent with that of Stevenson.

But Frankena seems to attribute a different view to Hutcheson. Frankena insists in various passages that "moral judgments are based on reasons." Now the phrase "based on reasons" may mean simply, as Stevenson might argue, that there are "reasons for approving" which support and are causally related to our attitudes. Frankena seems to mean something other than this when he claims that "the moral sense does base its judgments on reason."[46] He seems to be suggesting that a justifying reason is a reason why something is worthy of being approved. And if this is the case, then propositions about benevolent motives will be the reasons for holding that an act is worthy of approval. This is quite dif-

[45] Frankena, "Hutcheson's Moral Sense Theory," p. 374.
[46] *Ibid.*, p. 373.

ferent from the view attributed to Hutcheson in the long quotation above, according to which "a final justifying reason simply is a proposition to which the moral sense reacts favorably as such." [47] In the latter case, propositions about benevolent motives will be reasons to which the moral sense has reacted favorably. William T. Blackstone seems to agree with Frankena in holding that Hutcheson offers, not merely causal explanations, but grounds or reasons for moral judgments. Blackstone says of Hutcheson that "the ground or reason which he considers to be a justifying one for moral approval is that the motive of an act or person who performs the act is benevolent." [48]

If Blackstone and Frankena do indeed mean that propositions about benevolent motives are justifying reasons for holding that acts or persons are *worthy* of approval, then I believe that they are mistaken. The sort of view which they are attributing to Hutcheson makes him close to the so-called "good reasons" approach. Blackstone recognizes this and cites Bernard Peach [49] as holding that Hutcheson's position is like the "good reasons" approach. I should hold, on the contrary, that Hutcheson's theory is not that of the "good reasons" position, although, as I shall show, there are some similarities between them.

Let us therefore try to discover just what sort of theory of moral reasoning Hutcheson is maintaining. He says, again and again, that justifying reasons presuppose a moral sense. Such statements as the following are typical: "Now we shall find that all existing reasons presuppose instincts and affections; and the justifying presuppose a moral sense." [50] The appeal to the approval or disapproval of the moral sense is the end of the line for justification. There is no sense in which justifying reasons certify that some object is *worthy* of approval. They simply consist of statements about qualities or characteristics which are as a matter of fact approved. Indeed, strictly speaking, the approval of the moral sense is the source of all justification.

The view of justification which is here ascribed to Hutcheson is also to be found in Hume. Needless to say, the fact that Hume holds this view is no argument for ascribing it to Hutcheson. However, that Hume does hold it is of considerable interest because of the fact that he is so often found to be clarifying and adapting to his own use views which he must

---

[47] *Ibid.*, p. 374.

[48] Blackstone, *Francis Hutcheson and Contemporary Ethical Theory*, p. 30.

[49] Bernard Peach, "Francis Hutcheson and the Problem of Justification," an unpublished paper read at the Joint Philosophy Colloquium between Duke University and the University of North Carolina, December, 1956.

[50] Hutcheson, *Illustrations*, p. 218.

have read in Hutcheson. In the following passage, the view which I have
been ascribing to Hutcheson is ascribed to Hume by Ardal:

... when we have a certain peculiar sort of feeling, which we call a feeling
of blame, on contemplating a certain action or individual's character, no
more need be present in the situation in order that we may be justified in
pronouncing the action or the character vicious.[51]

It must surely be granted that this is a curious conception of justification.
I propose to consider in some detail, therefore, the conception of justification held by Hutcheson, although it is likely that most of my comments
might also be applied to Hume.

Hutcheson's employment of the term "approval" is again of central
importance. Attention has already been drawn to the way in which he
began by referring to the pleasure of which the moral sense is the source
and how he came to prefer the word "approval" for this sort of pleasure.
But what sort of feeling would approval have to be? On this view, we
would discover upon introspection a feeling of approval and might then,
if we were reflectively inclined, give thought to the actions or character-
dispositions which gave rise to this feeling. Feelings of approval might
well be more to inspection than the beliefs upon which they causally
depend. If approval is regarded as logically separated from its objects,
there is no limit to the "weird moral views," [52] as Phillipa Foot calls
them, which might be advocated. Approval might surely be directed towards mass murder, infanticide, flagpole sitting, etc., without contra-
diction. That such "weird moral views" are in the minority must then be
ascribed to the tendency to uniformity in human nature.

In short, the non-cognitivist theory under consideration, like the Subjective Theory, presents an erroneous account of moral approval. If,
on the one hand, approval were to be taken to connote judgment or
endorsement, then in approving we would be claiming that the act or
object in question comes up to certain standards. If, on the other hand,
approval is taken to be an emotion, as Hutcheson indeed takes it, then
this feeling is not in itself constitutive of the moral characteristic in question. Moore once stated that by approving of something we mean *"feeling
that it has a certain predicate* – the predicate, namely, which defines the
peculiar sphere of Ethics." [53] Without adopting Moore's intuitionism,
the related point might be made that Hutcheson's error is to attempt an
introspectionistic report of approval which, in sundering it from its logical

---

[51] Ardal, *Passion and Value,* p. 203.
[52] Philippa Foot, "Hume on Moral Judgment," in *David Hume: A Symposium,*
ed. by D. F. Pears (London: Macmillan & Co. Ltd., 1963), p. 71.
[53] Moore, *Principia Ethica,* p. 60.

connection with acts and character-dispositions, renders it constitutive of the moral characteristic. It is this same sort of error which Philippa Foot attributes to Hume. He is mistaken, she claims, when he appeals to a special feeling in trying to explain what it means to say that an action or quality is virtuous, for, as she puts it, "the explanation of the thought comes into the description of the feeling, not the other way round." [54]

Having pointed out certain objections to Hutcheson's treatment of the concept of approval, it must be added that there is a part of his theory of justification which needs to be singled out for attention, namely, that part according to which reasons for approving consist of statements to the effect that the approval follows the taking of the point of view of the spectator who is vividly imaginative, fully informed, impartial, and so on. In the preceding discussion, I ascribed to Hutcheson the view that propositions about benevolent motives are justifying reasons, not in the sense that they supply grounds for arguing that the act in question is worthy of approval, but only in the sense that the benevolence indicated by such propositions is as a matter of fact, approved. In this respect Hutcheson is therefore in essential agreement with Stevenson's treatment of the expression "reason for approving," although, unlike Stevenson, he believes that there is ultimately only one such reason, namely, benevolence. In view of Hutcheson's treatment of those propositions about benevolence which serve as justifying reasons, might we not treat in similar fashion those reasons for approving which consist of statements to the effect that the person viewing an act does so from the point of view of the impartial spectator?

We might expect that Hutcheson would describe the latter sort of reasons as simply causal conditions for our having a feeling of approval. Rather surprisingly he does not. There are passages in which he seems to maintain that approval has logical conditions. Whereas liking or experiencing ordinary sort of pleasures do not necessarily presuppose reflection and judgment, approval clearly does. Futhermore approval requires that we view an act or object apart from our interested relationship to it. That these are logical conditions seems suggested by Hutcheson's own language when he says that an action which one is obliged to do is one that "every spectator or he himself upon reflection *must* [italics mine] approve." [55]

We are now in a position to summarize the answer to the question concerning exactly what Hutcheson means by justification in connection

---

[54] Foot, "Hume on Moral Judgment," p. 71.
[55] Hutcheson, *Illustrations,* p. 232.

with moral judgments. Hutcheson's view seems to suggest that it is the approval of the moral sense which is the source of all justification. Accordingly, we might say, as Ardal did of Hume, that our justification for pronouncing an act morally good or virtuous is the presence of a feeling of approval. However, on closer inspection, it is apparent that Hutcheson is maintaining that this feeling has certain logical conditions, namely, those requiring the standpoint of an impartial spectator. It is in this part of his theory that he is unlike Stevenson and nearer to a "good reasons" approach.

This conception of justification is certainly more defensible than that which simply equates justification with the having of a peculiar feeling. Criticism of Hutcheson's theory of justification may now move to another level. Let us suppose that Hutcheson has tied the feeling of approval to certain logical conditions, namely, those conditions defined by the responses of the impartial spectator. Are these conditions not only necessary, but sufficient? It must be granted that some limit has been put to the "weird moral views" which could be defended if approval were to be logically separated from its objects. The question arises as to whether or not there are further logical ties. May approval, even granting that it is the approval of an impartial spectator, be directed towards any object whatsoever, towards mass murder, infanticide, etc.? I shall argue that it cannot, but shall postpone suggestions as to a theory alternative to Hutcheson's until my last chapter.

The issues concerning justification and moral reasoning arose out of a wider discussion of the nature and function of moral judgments. Let us therefore review how the issues concerning justification are related to those concerning moral judgments. After all, Hutcheson might be interpreted as holding the sort of position just described as regards moral reasoning, but as holding at the same time that moral judgments are merely expressive of a unique sort of emotional reaction called "approval." But this is not exactly the case. Certain developments occur in Hutcheson's treatment of moral judgments which parallel developments which we outlined in his treatment of moral reasoning. Consider, for example, the analogy which he presents between our judgments based on sense perceptions and our moral judgments. The view which he presents in the *Illustrations* may be paraphrased briefly as follows: Although disease and abnormal conditions result in our having all sorts of strange perceptions, we do not base our judgments on these perceptions but on the ordinary and normal perceptions which we have when in good health. Similarly, our ideas of actions and our approval or disapproval of them are to be such as are gained when reason corrects the report of the senses about the natural tendencies of these actions, when reason corrects rash conclusions about the affections of the agent, and when the approbation or disapprobation is such as represents the general sense of mankind.[56]

Taken together, the sorts of passages we have been considering constitute a very attractive part of Hutcheson's theory. This part of his theory accounts plausibly for the ways in which variations in our private responses may be altered and corrected. He clearly implies that moral discourse must reflect and require this sort of correction. In doing so, he supplies the materials for the more extended treatment given to these issues by Hume. The latter refers again and again to the way in which moral discourse requires a language in which we express sentiments "common to all mankind" and how, in such cases, a man must "depart from his private and particular station, and must choose a point of view, common to him with others; . . ." [57] Although Hume states his position with greater clarity and thoroughness, there is no major point made in these references to moral discourse and the way in which our sentiments are corrected which is not found in Hutcheson.

This brings us back to a final comment on that part of Frankena's interpretation of Hutcheson's theory according to which the latter is said to maintain that the attitude expressed in moral judgments is a unique sort of pleasure and might be referred to as a "peculiarly moral attitude." Hutcheson no doubt maintains that moral judgments are expressive of approval. But more needs to be said. On his view, it is a requirement of moral discourse that the approval expressed be that which would be experienced by someone who adopted the point of view of the impartial spectator. In his theory of knowledge Hutcheson insists that it is a requirement of discourse that "we denominate objects" from the appearances they make to us when we are in a normal condition. And, he adds, "just so in our ideas of actions." [58] Another way of putting the matter is to say that moral judgments imply certain claims to the effect that reasons may be given, reasons which testify that the approval which is expressed is that which would be experienced by someone who took the viewpoint of the impartial spectator. Such a position would be close to a non-cognitivist position described by Brandt as follows:

. . . ethical language *claims, of the attitude which it expresses,* that it satisfies all the conditions which would be set, as a general policy for the endorsement

---

[56] Hutcheson, *Illustrations,* p. 287.
[57] David Hume, *Enquiries Concerning the Human Understanding and Concerning the Principles of Morals* (2d ed.; Oxford: Clarendon Press, 1902), p. 272.
[58] Hutcheson, *Illustrations,* p. 287.

of attitudes governing or appraising choices or actions, by anyone who was intelligent and factually informed and had thought through the problems of the possible different general policies for the endorsement of such attitudes.[59]

What is claimed on such a non-cognitivist view is thus roughly equivalent to what is asserted by that cognitivist interpretation of the moral sense theory which Broad referred to as the trans-subjective, dispositional form of the Subjective Theory.

We are now in a position to compare two non-cognitivist interpretations of Hutcheson. According to the one discussed in the immediately preceding paragraphs, moral judgments are expressive of approval, but at the same time include claims to the effects that the approval expressed is that of the ideal spectator. According to the other, the interpretation which was attributed to Frankena, moral judgments are expressive of a peculiar sort of pleasure, but are at the same time based on a justifying reason, namely, that the act or character-disposition is benevolent. It must be added that, according to the latter, a justifying reason is a proposition about some act or character-disposition which is worthy of approval. I have argued that the first of the above theories is that which most adequately represents Hutcheson's views. Furthermore, it seems to me that the non-cognitive theory which I have ascribed to Hutcheson is in many respects an extremely attractive theory.

However, serious criticisms may be directed against the latter theory which parallel the criticisms which Broad directed against the trans-subjective, dispositional form of the Subjective Theory. Broad sums up the difficulties of this theory in the following:

(i) Can it deal with the fact that judgments like "That act is right" seem always to be grounded upon the presence in the act of some non-ethical right-inclining characteristics, such as the fulfilment of a promise? (ii) If so, can it deal with the further fact that the connection between a right-inclining characteristic and the rightness which it tends to convey seems to be necessary and synthetic? And (iii) can it deal with the fact that it seems not only intelligible but also true to say that the moral pro-emotion is felt towards an act in respect of the characteristic of *rightness* and moral anti-emotion in respect of the characteristic of wrongness? [60]

Defenders of the moral sense theory, whether cognitivists or non-cognitivists, might of course argue the case on epistemological grounds, claiming that Broad's appeal to synthetic a priori judgments is indefensible. But, granting that it may be logically possible to rule out moral

---

[59] Richard B. Brandt, *Ethical Theory* (Englewood Cliffs, N.J.: Prentice-Hall, Inc., 1959), p. 268.
[60] Broad, "Moral-Sense Theories in Ethics," p. 376.

theories on epistemological grounds, such a practice fails to satisfy our interest in solving the problems in the particular context in which they occur. What is needed, therefore, is an examination of Hutcheson's account of the relationship between ethical characteristics and those non-ethical characteristics which Broad calls "right-inclining."

In many respects, this examination has already been conducted. In brief, let us consider its results as applied to the theory which I have ascribed to Hutcheson. According to this theory, there are certain logical requirements to be met by moral judgments. These have to do with the fact that there are certain implicit claims about the attitudes expressed by moral judgments. In a certain sense, one might hold that it is a "right-inclining characteristic" of moral judgments that a certain standpoint is taken, namely, that of an ideal spectator, and that it is to this rather complex characteristic that approval is necessarily connected. This sort of move, however, is only partly satisfactory. What Broad clearly has in mind is rather the relationship, on such a theory as Hutcheson's, of benevolence to ethical characteristics. And on this score, the answer is that on Hutcheson's theory this relationship is contingent, not necessary. Broad, at this point, would argue that, on the contrary, the connection between such a right-inclining characteristic – assuming that it is indeed right-inclining – and rightness is necessary and synthetic.

Without pursuing Broad's own arguments for the presence of non-natural qualities, we may return to some difficulties which we found earlier in connection with Hutcheson's treatment of approval, the feeling expressed in moral judgments. Earlier, we saw how his introspectionist treatment of approval sunders it from its logical connection with acts and character-dispositions. If, therefore, moral judgments are held to express approval, then statements about benevolent acts or character-dispositions can only be contingently related to such judgments. Such a theory, we have argued, seems inadequate in failing to reflect characteristics of moral discourse and moral reasoning.

The interpretation of Hutcheson advanced by Frankena does recognize that reasons may be given for moral judgments and is therefore a theory which might be elaborated in such a fashion as to escape some of the criticisms which I have levelled against the theory which I believe Hutcheson to have actually held. But I shall postpone until the last chapter further suggestions as to how the theory which Hutcheson holds might be improved and shall continue, in the next chapter, to examine some further characteristics of this theory.

CHAPTER III

THE MORAL SENSE AND MOTIVATION

Morality is practical; it shapes, guides and directs behavior. It is doubtful that any philosopher has ever disagreed with the foregoing claims. Disagreement arises, however, when we press for further specification of just how morality is practical and how it provides this influence. In this chapter I intend to examine and evaluate Hutcheson's position as regards this question of how morality is practical.

But before turning to Hutcheson, I wish to consider briefly some aspects of the conceptual framework in which this problem is located.

A number of contemporary writers have devoted close attention to the relationship between moral judgments and motivation. Among these are Prichard, Falk, Nowell-Smith, and Frankena. Emerging from the articles by Falk [1] and Frankena [2] are two terms, "externalism" and "internalism," which help to clarify the issues with which I shall be concerned. The term "externalist" is used to describe those who maintain, in Frankena's terms, that "it is in some sense logically possible for an agent to have or see that he has an obligation even if he has no motivation, actual or dispositional, for doing the act in question." [3] For example, an intuitionist might maintain that obligation is a non-natural characteristic and that it does not follow from our knowing that we are obliged that we have any motivation whatsoever. "Internalism," on the other hand, is described by Frankena as the view that it would be paradoxical or even logically impossible for an agent to have an obligation without having some motive for doing what he is obliged to do. For example, Stevenson expresses an internalist

[1] W. D. Falk, "'Ought' and Motivation," in *Readings in Ethical Theory*, ed. by Wilfrid Sellars and John Hospers (New York: Appleton-Century-Crofts, Inc., 1952).
[2] William K. Frankena, "Obligation and Motivation in Recent Moral Philosophy," in *Essays in Moral Philosophy*, ed. by A. I. Melden (Seattle: University of Washington Press, 1958).
[3] *Ibid.*, p. 40.

theory when he claims that the ethical term "goodness" must have a "magnetism" and that, as he goes on to state, "a person who recognizes X to be 'good' must *ipso facto* acquire a stronger tendency to act in its favor than he otherwise would have had." [4]

If one turns to the moral philosophies of Hutcheson and Hume, nothing seems so well-documented as their claims that morality is dynamic and that moral judgments must be capable of influencing us to action. These claims, not always explicit, constitute an underlying background for Hutcheson's theory. In Hume, these claims are stated explicitly and emphatically in the very opening passages of Book III of the *Treatise*. These passages, so central for Hume's entire theory, proclaim that morality is practical, that "morals excite passions, and produce or prevent actions." [5] Yet is appears to me that few important doctrines have been so ill-documented as regards a truly careful study of exactly how, according to Hutcheson and Hume, moral judgments are practical and dynamic.

Turning, then, to Hutcheson, it would seem that his moral philosophy tends towards "internalism," the view that motivation is inherent in the very nature of moral judgments. Rachael Kydd seems to take this interpretation of Hutcheson when she ascribes to him the position that "judgments about the obligatoriness of acts must provide the agent with 'exciting reasons' for doing them" and that "judgments which verify moral propositions must also be capable of influencing us to action." [6] In reading Hutcheson one is certainly struck by the fact that he inherits from Shaftesbury what might be called an "internalistic mood." In Shaftesbury, morality and religion are not to be thought of as calculations of the sorts of future rewards and punishments depicted by the egoists. Shaftesbury describes morality, not in terms of the path of greatest resistance, but as shot through with intrinsic appeal, attractiveness, and delight. The following statement is typical:

[The mind] feels the soft, the harsh, the agreeable and disagreeable in the affections; and finds a foul and a fair, a harmonious and dissonant, as really and truly here as in any musical number or in the outward forms or representations of sensible things. Nor can it withhold its admiration and ecstacy, its aversion and scorn, any more in what relates to one than to the other of these subjects. [7]

---

[4] Charles L. Stevenson, "The Emotive Meaning of Ethical Terms," in *Readings in Ethical Theory*, ed. by Wilfrid Sellers and John Hospers (New York: Appleton-Century-Crofts, Inc., 1952), p. 417.
[5] Hume, *Treatise*, p. 457.
[6] Kydd, *Reason and Conduct*, p. 39.
[7] Shaftesbury, *Characteristics*, I, 251.

Steeped in this sort of passage, Hutcheson must have been persuaded that morality is intensely practical, dynamic, and moving. However, critics are agreed that Shaftesbury is notoriously obscure, if not inconsistent, with respect to a clear statement of such basic issues as how we come to know the right and how we are motivated to perform right actions.

How Hutcheson develops his own position can best be seen in terms of his criticism of two theories which he rejects as inadequate, namely ethical egoism and ethical rationalism. It seems evident that Hutcheson regards the ethical egoists as holding a form of "internalism" according to which to be obliged is to have a motive. Among the senses of the word "obligation" Hutcheson distinguishes that sense by which we understand "a motive from self-interest, sufficient to determine all those who duly consider it, and pursue their own advantage wisely, to a certain course of actions." [8] The ethical egoist is correct enough in recognizing this use of the term "obligation." Furthermore he is correct, from Hutcheson's point of view, in his assumption that to be obliged, in this sense, is to have a motive. Morality, for both Hutcheson and the ethical egoist, is practical and dynamic. The error of the egoist lies in the fact that he supposes the above to be the one and only sense of the term "obligation." Hutcheson, as we shall see, can proceed to establish at least one other sense of the term "obligation" without giving up the view that to be obliged is to have some motive or other.

The rationalist, as compared with the egoist, presents a theory which is much more offensive to Hutcheson as regards the problem of the relationship of morality to motivation. It is therefore necessary to discuss in considerable detail his criticisms of the rationalists.

HUTCHESON'S CRITICISMS OF THE RATIONALISTS

In all of his attacks upon the rationalists, it is Samuel Clarke whom Hutcheson has mainly in mind. What, then, does Clarke have to say concerning our knowledge of right and wrong and of the way in which we are influenced to action by this knowledge. It would be wholly incorrect to say that Clarke was unappreciative of the sort of comment to be made later by Hume who said "'tis one thing to know virtue, and another to conform the will to it." [9] Clarke is perfectly aware of the fact that one may know the right and yet fail to conform the will to this knowledge. What he does maintain is that "'tis as natural and (morally speaking)

---

[8] Selby-Bigge, *British Moralists,* I, 154.
[9] Hume, *Treatise,* p. 465.

necessary, that the will should be determined in every action by the reason of the thing, and the right of the case, as 'tis natural and (absolutely speaking) necessary, that the understanding should submit to a demonstrated truth." [10] Clarke distinguishes between what he calls "secondary" obligation, that obligation which is grounded in the sanctions of rewards and punishments, and the "truest and formallest" obligation grounded in the "eternal reason of things." Although "obligation" is not equated with "rightness," the logical connections between the terms are unquestioned by Clarke. The right and "fitting" ought to be done. "These eternal and necessary difference of things," he states, "make it fit and reasonable for creatures so to act; they cause it to be their duty, or lay an obligation upon them, so to do; . . ." [11] In this and similar passages Clarke maintains that to know what is right is to know what is fitting and, at the same time, to be obliged to act accordingly, apart from considerations of self-interest.

As regards the relationship of thought to action, Clarke ascribes reasonableness not only to judgments about rightness, but also to actions which are governed by our judgment of what is right. Clarke may well grant that it is one thing to call a judgment "reasonable" and another to apply this term to actions. The progression of his thought is presumably this: rightness and wrongness are characteristics that can only be known through reason. Furthermore, the belief that an action is right is, sometimes at least, a motive for doing it. Hence, since this motive depends upon reason for its existence, actions performed from it may be called "reasonable." Opponents of Clarke, such as Hutcheson, will of course deny both his premises and his conclusion.

There are the causes, according to Clarke, of our acting unreasonably, namely "negligent misunderstanding" and "wilful passions or lusts." [12] Let us consider these in turn. By the first, "negligent misunderstanding," Clarke refers to a theoretical failure. At one point Clarke presses the analogy between moral knowledge and sight, declaring that to deny those truths which reason apprehends is as if a man who beholds the sun were to deny the existence of light. If rightness is an intuited characteristic, then moral disagreement or error may be explained as a failure to distinguish this characteristic, a failure which may be ascribed to a sort of blindness in those who are mature and, in those who are not, to their lack of development or, as in the case of mental defectives, to their utter moral incapacity.

[10] Samuel Clarke, *Discourse Upon Natural Religion,* in Selby-Bigge, *British Moralists,* II, 13.
[11] *Ibid.,* II, 3.
[12] *Ibid.,* II, 13.

The sort of theoretical failure which we have been describing has been frequently appealed to by followers of the intuitionist tradition. What is of peculiar interest is that Clarke, although he takes note of this sort of error, is far more preoccupied with a different sort of "negligent misunderstanding." He pursues, somewhat stridently, an analogy with mathematical truth which leads him to maintain that to mistake negligently right and wrong may be compared to believing that twice two is equal to five. A man who willfully acts contrary to justice "wills things to be what they are not and cannot be." [13] Sidgwick suggests that Clarke may be interpreted as meaning, less paradoxically, that the will should be determined in every action by the reason of the thing and that "if a man deviates from the rules of Equity and Universal Benevolence . . . it is not, in Clarke's view, that he has solid reasons for so deviating, but that he is partly under the influence of irrational impulses." [14] But Sidgwick is here expunging a feature of Clarke's theory, granted that it is a troublesome feature. Again, let us attend to Clarke:

'Tis as absurd and blameworthy to mistake negligently plain right and wrong, that is, to understand the proportions of things in morality to be what they are not, or wilfully to act contrary to known justice and equity, that is, to will things to be what they are not and cannot be, as it would be absurd and ridiculous for a man in arithmetical matters, ignorantly to believe that twice two is not equal four, or wilfully and obstinately to contend, *against his own clear knowledge* [italics mine], that the whole is not equal to all its parts.[15]

By his above use of the phrase "against our clear knowledge" Clarke seems to suggest that all moral agents have a clear knowledge of moral truths. That this is the case in all circumstances is surely to be doubted. It is only with respect to the most artificial sort of examples, best taken out of context, that we can have this sort of assurance of our knowledge of moral truths. And surely such "clear knowledge" would have to be in some sense dispositional, rather than occurrent, in those cases where "negligent misunderstanding" takes place.

According to Clarke, reasonable actions are those which are governed by our judgment of what is right. To be sure, this is a use of the term "reasonable" which cannot be identified with "reasoning." It presupposes that it is reason which discloses the presence of moral characteristics. Unreasonable acts caused by "negligent misunderstanding" are thus actions which are governed by our mistaken judgments of what is right.

[13] *Ibid.*
[14] Henry Sidgwick, *Outline of the History of Ethics* (London: Macmillan and Co., Limited, 1949), p. 182.
[15] Selby-Bigge, *British Moralists*, II, 14.

If we grant for the moment this interpretation of reasonable and unreasonable acts, how are we to interpret Clarke's statements that in
acting wrongly we are guilty of a sort of absurdity and of willing things
to be what they are not. Just as "reasonable" cannot be equated with
"reasoning" in any strict formal, logical sense, so Clarke's suggestions
that actions are self-contradictory must be interpreted somewhat gener-
ously in order to make sense out of them. Actions, it must be granted,
cannot contradict one another in any straightforward sense. The un-
reasonableness of acting contrary to one's beliefs cannot be described in
any strict sense as a logical error. What occurs, in Clarke's opinion, is
presumably something like this: in acting we sometimes, if not always,
perform acts because we believe them to be right or "fitting." If, therefore, we perform a wrong act, we are performing it in the mistaken belief
that it is right. Now since, in Clarke's opinion, such mistakes are negligent
and made in spite of the clear knowledge which we really in some sense
have, we might find ourselves willing both that an act be performed and
that it not be performed. In such cases, Clarke would maintain, we are
guilty of inconsistency and self-contradiction in our acts.

Clarke's second cause of unreasonable action, the operation of "wilful
lusts and passions," receives from him a rather traditional treatment.
Reason is depicted as being deflected from its course by impulse. In this
case we may have a clear knowledge of where our duty lies, but nevertheless fail to do it. In a moral agent, therefore, reason must subdue the
passions.

Most really interesting philosophical controversies have their origin
in the fact that some philosopher or group of philosophers holds un-
critically to some doctrine which arouses in others a sense of puzzlement
and unease. It has been characteristic of intuitionists that, perhaps with
the exception of his contention that acts may be self-contradictory, they
find no sense of unease in the sort of doctrines promulgated by Clarke.
Sidgwick, in many ways the most astute of them all, exemplifies this lack
of puzzlement. He proceeds at one point to describe what he admits to
be the peculiarities of moral cognition. But he goes on soon after to confess
that if this doctrine of ethical judgments is accepted together with his
belief that "such judgments are inseparably combined with an impulse
to action of a peculiar kind," then, as he puts it "the question whether
a bare cognition or any purely intellectual operation can or cannot influence volition, does not seem to me one of practical importance, however interesting it may be from a psychological point of view." [16] One of

[16] Sidgwick, *Methods of Ethics,* p. 31.

Hutcheson's great contributions is that he gives expression to the puzzlement and unease which some have felt at these sorts of doctrines as presented by intuitionists like Clarke and Sidgwick.

Hutcheson's criticisms of the rationalists tend to fall into two categories: (1)(arguments against their view that reason can move to action; (2) arguments, mainly epistemological, which attempt to show that their appeals to "fittingness" are indefensible and that moral distinctions have their origins in a moral sense. Let us proceed to consider these in turn. Some philosophical movements, in the process of their development, come to employ a number of terms which are useful for plugging conceptual gaps and yet are themselves in need of careful definition. The ethical rationalists of the seventeenth century had a fairly large number of such terms and phrases in their vocabulary. Included among them were such expressions as "conformity to truth," "acting suitable to the nature of things," "conformity to reason," "congruity and incongruity between actions and relations," and "conformity to the fitness of things." Granted that these expressions had been criticized by some philosophers, it was Hutcheson who presented the most sustained and critical examination of these terms as employed by the rationalists.

Hutcheson begins by trying to discover what meaning can be attached to the description of actions as "conforming to reason." He joins Burnet, one of his rationalist opponents, in defining reason as our power of finding out true propositions.[17] Hutcheson quickly rules out one sort of conformity, namely, the "conformity which is between every true proposition and its object."[18] He maintains that the latter sort of conformity, or as we might call it, correspondence with fact, is found in all actions alike. The latter claim seems somewhat obscure. What he means is explained in the sentences following the above quotation which point out that true statements can be made about any action whatsoever. How then can we distinguish between the worth of actions when all conform to truth, that is, when true propositions can be made of each and every one of them?

The latter point seems so obvious that it is hard to imagine that anyone would disagree. Yet Hutcheson must have had in mind one philosopher in particular, William Wollaston, who held a very curious and extreme position according to which those actions are right which conform to truth. Whereas in dealing with the epistemology of morals, Hutcheson's criticisms of the rationalists are directed mostly at Samuel Clarke,

---

[17] In Chapter II I attempted to explain how Hutcheson could maintain that reason is our power of finding out true propositions and at the same time be committed to an empirical epistemology.

[18] Hutcheson, *Illustrations*, 215.

in dealing with what might be called the psychology of morals, Hutcheson often singles out Wollaston as the target for his most sustained criticisms, although it might be argued that here too the inspiring force behind Wollaston is Clarke. Wollaston follows Clarke in advocating the rather extreme view which we discussed earlier to the effect that wrong acts are somehow self-contradictory and involve a willing that things both be and not be. But, we might observe, self-contradiction in its most literal sense can only be ascribed to propositions. Wollaston here takes a most unusual view. In its milder form his position is that actions imply propositions. In his strongest form, his position is that acts *are* propositions. Wollaston maintains: "if that proposition, which is false, be wrong, that act which implies such a proposition, or is founded upon it cannot be right." The words "implies" and "is founded upon" are consistent with a milder theory. But he goes on to declare of an act such as the latter that "it is the very proposition itself in practice," [19] and seems here to embrace the strong interpretation of his theory.

Wollaston has been much attacked for the "queerheaded" moral theory he proposes. What he is groping towards, in my opinion, is a clear statement of the relationship between thought and action. The experiences which give rise to his theory are quite recognizable. In making statements we often make implicit contextual claims that our statements are defensible. Similarly, in saying that "actions speak louder than words," we suggest that in performing actions, we often do so together with the implicit claim that such actions are defensible, that reasons could be given for them. Sir Leslie Stephen, in criticizing Wollaston, states: "Thirty years of profound meditation had convinced Wollaston that the reason why a man should abstain from breaking his wife's head was, that it was denying she was his wife." [20] But might not someone who performs an act do so with the implicit claim that he had good reason for so doing? When I throw the ball to second base, I am able to defend my act with a justifying reason, e.g., that, as pitcher, I saw a runner trying to steal to second. Might not a similar type of explanation be applied to the quotation from Sir Leslie Stephen? That is, if someone were deliberately and not impulsively to break his wife's head, would this act not claim that some justifying reason could be given for it? And indeed, justifying reasons could be imagined, e.g. she deserved to be beaten, she was hysterical and needed to be "snapped out of it," etc. However, it is more

[19] William Wollaston, *The Religion of Nature Delineated*, in Selby-Bigge, British Moralists, II, 364.
[20] Sir Leslie Stephen, *History of English Thought in the Eighteenth Century* (2 vols.; New York: G. P. Putnam's Sons, 1902), I, 130.

plausible to restrict Wollaston's theory to cases of acts which fall under descriptions with a built-in eulogistic or dyslogistic force. For example, it might be maintained that, in a normal context, such expressions as "beating one's wife" or "murdering one's wife" include a built-in dyslogistic force tying them to assumptions that the acts in question are wrong.

Although, as I have suggested, one can appreciate the nature of the problems raised by Wollaston concerning the relationship of thought to action, his theory bristles with difficulties and obscurities which render it of little value. Hutcheson exposes most if not all of these difficulties. Hutcheson's comments on the phrase "conformity to truth" serve to remind Wollaston – and indeed any others who use this phrase carelessly – that we can formulate all sorts of true propositions which have nothing to do with virtue. "Is it virtue to say at Christmas, that the mornings are sharp?" [21] asks Hutcheson. It is evident that even if the truth of some propositions were a necessary criterion for the morality of an action, this alone could not provide a sufficient criterion. This argument is valid not only against Wollaston but against Clarke and other rationalists. This is in fact admitted by a later and more subtle rationalist, Richard Price, who says of such phrases as "conforming to truth" that "these expressions are of no use, and have little meaning, if considered as intended to *define* virtue; for they evidently *presuppose* it." [22]

The foregoing comments are also relevant to Wollaston's claim that wrong-doing involves self-contradiction or that moral evil is acting a lie. Wollaston, as Hutcheson claims, must first establish the nature of moral evil. If Wollaston appeals, as Clarke would, to the apprehension of moral truths through reason, then Hutcheson counters with his empiricist interpretation of the origin and nature of moral concepts. And, even if Wollaston were able to establish the existence of moral truths, he would still not have shown the logical or causal relationship between knowledge of such truths and motivation. Deficient in these various respects, Wollaston's remarks on reasonableness and self-contradiction in action are valueless. It might be added that as regards his interest in the relationship of thought to action, Wollaston is obscure in other ways which Hutcheson did not concern himself with, but which have aroused critical comment from Hume and later commentators. Such critics have argued that actions cannot contradict one another in any straightforward sense. Nor can the

---

[21] Hutcheson, *Illustrations,* p. 266.
[22] Richard Price, *A Review of the Principal Questions in Morals,* ed. by D. Daiches Raphael (Oxford: Clarendon Press, 1948), p. 125.

failure to act on one's beliefs be considered to be a strictly logical error. And in what sense are acts incompatible? To these and other related questions Wollaston's theory affords no clear and helpful answer.

Having traced some of Hutcheson's criticisms of the rationalists with respect to the problem of how reason can move to action, let us see how he formulates his own theory. In their most compressed form, Hutcheson's arguments in the *Illustrations* might be said to proceed along the following lines. His opening argument regarding the phrase "conformity to truth" serves as an introduction to his more central contention that truths, no matter what their subject matter, cannot move to action. Whatever it might mean to "conform our actions to true propositions," this can never mean that any true proposition is itself capable of moving us to action. And reason, which he has here defined as our power of finding out true propositions, cannot, as an independent variable, move us to action.

Let us see how Hutcheson works these arguments into his theory. From statements which present our reasons for believing, or acting, or indeed for anything whatsoever, it is an easy transition to postulate the existence of reason as a faculty which is the source of all such reasons. A theory which proceeded to make such a transition would be inclined to look for homogeneity in the various reasons which we find given in ordinary discourse. Hutcheson, in resisting such a transition, dwells instead on the differences which exist in the reasons we give. These reasons, however, he finds to be of two types, "exciting reasons" and "justifying reasons." The former he says, "presuppose instincts and affections"; the latter "presuppose a moral sense." The following passage is extremely central and repays close study:

When we ask the reason of an action, we sometimes mean, "what truth shows a quality in the action, exciting the agent to do it?" Thus, why does a luxurious man pursue wealth? The reason is given by this truth, "Wealth is useful to purchase pleasures." Sometimes for a reason of actions we shew the truth expressing a quality, engaging our approbation. Thus the reason of hazarding life in a just war, is, that "it tends to preserve our honest countrymen, or evidences public spirit": ... The former sort of reasons we will call *exciting* and the latter *justifying*.[23]

When an action is said to "conform to reason" this could only mean, according to Hutcheson, either that there is an exciting reason for the action or that there is a justifying reason for the action. He believes himself to be a follower of Aristotle in maintaining that there are ultimate

[23] Hutcheson, *Illustrations*, p. 218.

ends desired without a view to anything else and that we deliberate, not about these ends, but about means to them. Ultimate ends presuppose instincts and affections. Actions, therefore, cannot be called "reasonable" in any sense which would suggest that their ends are determined by reason alone. "What is reason," he asks in the *Inquiry*, "but that sagacity we have in prosecuting any end?" [24] In the *Illustrations* he expands this in declaring:

He acts reasonably, who considers the various actions in his power, and forms true opinions of their tendencies; and then chooses to do that which will obtain the highest degree of that, to which the instincts of his nature incline him, with the smallest degree of those things from which the affections in his nature make him averse.[25]

How, in view of this position regarding reasonable acts, could such acts ever have come to be so utterly contrasted with actions which are from affections and passions? Hutcheson suggests that this may be explained by the fact that some of our actions are motivated by calm desires which are guided by reason whereas others are impulsive, violent, or passionate. Actions motivated by calm desires have come to be called "reasonable." To parody Hume, we might say that, for Hutcheson, reason is, if not the slave, certainly the servant of the calm desires. As noted earlier, Hume's term "calm passion" could not be used by Hutcheson since it would contain a self-contradiction. According to Hutcheson, passions are inherently violent. Against the rationalists, it might be added that, for Hutcheson, an act may be reasonable in his sense of the term without being virtuous or moral.

Attention should be drawn to the fact that the reasonableness of those actions which are motivated by calm desires is a reasonableness ascribable only to their exciting reasons. There is no sense in which reasonableness can be ascribed to actions just because they are guided or governed by justifying reasons issuing from our moral sense.

Before returning in the next section to a lengthier study of justifying reasons and their relationship to motivation, let us pause to ask how Hutcheson's analysis of exciting and justifying reasons serves to promote his cause against the rationalists. At this point the rationalist might interject that accepting the distinction between exciting and justifying reasons does not coerce us into the further conclusion that this justifying reason has its source in a moral sense. The rationalist might even grant that approval is present whenever we discover justifying reasons and might present his

[24] Selby-Bigge, *British Moralists*, I, 115.
[25] Hutcheson, *Illustrations*, p. 226.

own explanation of the presence of approval. He might observe that the term "approval" suffers from vagueness and ambiguity. In one sense, the term "approval" means to judge according to some standard. In another, it connotes an emotion or feeling, as, for example, when we speak of "feeling approval." But, says the rationalist, these difficulties involved in using the term "approval" may be resolved if we suppose that reason provides a standard for approval through its intuitive knowledge of moral characteristics. As to the element of feeling, he might claim, rather simply, that such feelings of approval are present when we recognize moral truths. Or he might hold the more subtle position, once suggested by C. D. Broad, that although right, good, and ought are sui generis, a priori, and known by reason, the occasions for the formation of such a priori concepts are feelings of approval and disapproval.[26]

It is at this point that Hutcheson brings forth his arguments to the effect that moral distinctions have their sources, not, as the rationalists held, in an apprehension of "fittingness," but in a moral sense. Hutcheson grants that the word "fitting" may be applied to means, but challenges the application of this word to ends themselves. As regards "fitness" as the ultimate moral characteristic he asks:

What means the fitness of an ultimate end? For what is it fit? Why, it is an ultimate end, not fit for any thing farther, but absolutely fit. What means that word fit? If it notes a simple idea it must be the perception of some sense: thus we must recur, upon this scheme too, to a moral sense.[27]

With the foregoing passage we arrive at a crucial point in Hutcheson's theory. As an empiricist, he must insist that all simple ideas have their origin in a sense. His philosophical opponents, such as Clarke, Price, and, more recently, Sidgwick and Moore, maintain the contrary. Nevertheless it is unfair to say of Hutcheson, as Raphael does, that he simply begs the question as to the origin of simple ideas.[28] Behind his appeals to a moral sense Hutcheson has the weight of a formidable empiricist epistemology which we have already treated in detail. And, in fairness to Hutcheson, it might be remarked that some of the developments of the rationalists' theories in men such as Richard Price became more subtle largely through their having to meet Hutcheson's attacks on earlier rationalists such as Clarke and Wollaston.

Let us pause to take an overview of the controversy between Hutcheson and the rationalists. If the rationalists had appreciated Hutcheson's

---

[26] Broad, *Five Types of Ethical Theory*, p. 270.
[27] Hutcheson, *Illustrations*, p. 255.
[28] Raphael, *The Moral Sense*, p. 40.

opening argument against their appeal to a "conformity to truth," they might have replied along the following lines: reason is indeed the power of finding true propositions. But such true propositions will include those which are about moral characteristics or "moral facts." In conforming to *these* true propositions which are discovered by reason, an action is reasonable. Nothing in Hutcheson's opening argument would serve to refute a rationalist who argued in this fashion. His opening argument merely has the force of showing that "conformity to truth," i.e. to any truth whatsoever, is not sufficient to provide a definition of virtue. Hutcheson must and does attempt to supply further arguments to support his conviction that reason cannot supply true propositions about moral characteristics.

What of his further argument that we are not moved simply by a knowledge of truths? He had agreed with the rationalists that reason is the power of finding true propositions. This agreement should not conceal an underlying difference. Hutcheson, following Locke, maintains that although a true proposition requires the perception of a relation of ideas, the ideas thus related are derived entirely from experience. Rationalists will of course disagree regarding this derivation. But, to go on, Hutcheson maintains that we are moved, not by true propositions alone, but by instincts. It is a truth, he says, that rhubarb strengthens the stomach, "but it is not a proposition which strengthens the stomach, but the quality in that medicine." [29] To my knowledge, no rationalist responded to this specific argument in Hutcheson, but surely we might suppose that a sophisticated rationalist such as Price might answer that it is an *ignoratio elenchi*. Granted that reason does not move us just by discovering true propositions, the rationalist might maintain that in addition to discovering true propostions reason serves to disclose moral characteristics and, in doing so, moves us to action. Hutcheson is maintaining that no truth can move to action merely because it is true. There must be some quality which is denoted by the true proposition and which moves us. But this is exactly what the rationalist might maintain. However, what needs to be emphasized is that there are two questions which must be distinguished. In the first place, the rationalist must establish that there are moral truths known by reason. In the second place, he must show how motivation is related to knowledge of this truth, even if the knowledge in question is of some non-natural characteristic such as Clarke's "fittingness." Seen in perspective, Hutcheson has contributed greatly to the clarification of these questions and has maintained, against the rationalist, that the source of

[29] Hutcheson, *Illustrations,* p. 221.

moral ideas must be a sense and that, as regards motivation, the rationalist must make explicit just how recognition of a moral truth would be logically or causally related to motivation.

Because the rationalists whom we have been discussing did not make explicit just how recognition of a moral truth is logically or causally related to motivation, it is not at all easy to locate their position with respect to the controversy between the internalists and externalists which was described at the beginning of this chapter. Everything depends on how the rationalist supposes that moral truths are practical – and that is precisely where he is most vague. Various interpretations of the rationalist position may be defended by appropriate quotations. The rationalist may be interpreted, for example, as holding that knowledge of the right lays an obligation upon us. This is like knowledge of a peculiar "fact," a fact which might be said to have obligatoriness "built into it." This sort of interpretation is easily supported by those many passages in Clarke in which he indicates that the "right" and "fitting" ought to be done. But, again, how does the recognition that some act ought to be done relate to motivation. Here again Clarke fails to provide clarification.

In order to compare the position of the rationalists with that of Hutcheson it is of interest to outline briefly some of the directions which rationalists and intuitionists might take. Frankena maintains that intuitionism is the most striking example of "externalism." [30] On this interpretation, a moral judgment asserts a kind of fact. No reference to conation is involved in such a judgment and nothing follows logically as regards motivation. It would be possible for someone to know the right and yet have no motive for acting accordingly. Most externalists, however, would probably hold that the knowledge provided by reason or intuition does as a matter of fact arouse in us a desire, usually identified with the desire to do the right. This is the view defended by Sir W. D. Ross who holds that not only a desire to do our duty, but other desires, such as the desire to understand, are desires which, as he says; "could not have existed if we were not rational beings." [31] This sort of view may take the form which maintains that the desire awakened by reason is, as Sidgwick maintains, "an impulse to action of a peculiar kind, which it is necessary to distinguish from non-rational desires of inclinations." [32] Or, it might make no distinction between the desire awakened by reason and other garden-variety desires.

[30] Frankena, "Obligation and Motivation," p. 43.
[31] Sir W. David Ross, *Foundations of Ethics* (Oxford: Clarendon Press, 1939), p. 205.
[32] Sidgwick, *Methods of Ethics,* p. 31.

Although Frankena is quite right in contending that intuitionism is, generally speaking, a striking example of externalism, one finds upon close inspection that there are positions maintained by intuitionists which are not readily labelled "externalist." Prichard at one time defended the view that "desire and the sense of obligation are coordinate forms or species of motive." [33] This position of Prichard's is surely a type of internalism, since to assent to a moral judgment is in this case to have a kind of motivation, although not to be moved by desire. In claiming that there can be motivation without desire such a position is of course in direct opposition to the tradition of Hutcheson and Hume.

Another intuitionist position not readily labelled "externalist" without qualification is that of Sidgwick who maintains that moral judgments concerning the obligatory or the right are "inseparably combined with an impulse to action of a peculiar kind, which it is necessary to distinguish from non-rational desires or inclinations." [34] The words "inseparably combined" are worth stressing. Does Sidgwick, who is logically sophisticated and most careful of his terminology, really mean that from such moral judgments it "logically follows" that there is an impulse to action? Closely related to Sidgwick on this point is Price's contention that "when we are conscious that an act is *fit* to be done . . . it is not conceivable that we can remain *uninfluenced* or want a *motive* to action." [35]

Upon close examination we find, therefore, that some of the most important intuitionists do not hold clearly definable externalist positions according to which it is simply a contingent fact that in human beings cognition of the right or obligatory arouses desire. But let us turn now to see what alternatives are offered by Hutcheson's theory.

THE MORAL SENSE AND MOTIVATION

Having followed Hutcheson's criticisms of the egoists and rationalists, it is of interest to see whether or not he can construct an ethical theory which offers a plausible alternative. I shall be especially concerned with the problem of how, according to his theory, the moral sense is related to motivation and with the related problem of how moral judgments are practical.

It is important to raise these issues in the context of Hutcheson's own terminology. A good place to start is with the question: do justifying

[33] H. A. Prichard, *Moral Obligation* (Oxford: Clarendon Press, 1949), p. 11.
[34] Sidgwick, *Methods of Ethics*, p. 31.
[35] Price, *Review*, p. 186.

reasons move us to action? Since, as it was shown earlier, justifying reasons presuppose and issue from the moral sense, this question concerns at the same time the relationhip of the moral sense to motivation. Commentators exhibit considerable disagreement in their interpretations of Hutcheson's answer to this question. Since their disagreement lends support to my claim that there is here a basic source of difficulty in Hutcheson's theory, I wish to devote some attention to their views.

Rachael Kydd ascribes to Hutcheson the position that, as she phrases it, "judgments about the obligatoriness of acts must provide the agent with 'exciting reasons' for doing them: and since exciting reasons cannot exist independently of our desires, and since desires are empirical facts, it follows that *a priori* reasoning cannot verify moral propositions." [36] Yet she complains a few lines later that "Hutcheson made it clear that judgments which verify moral propositions must also be capable of influencing us to action, but his analysis of these judgments remained obscure." [37] Now the judgments which verify moral propositions are what Hutcheson calls "justifying reasons." Therefore, if we compress the above comments, we seem to find Kydd saying that judgments about obligatoriness, hence judgments for which justifying reasons may be given, must also "excite," but that how this comes about is obscure or unclear. With this accusation I wholeheartedly agree. As regards obligation, Kydd makes the claim, speaking of Hutcheson, that "on this view it is clear that no act can rightly be called obligatory unless it can be shown that the agent has a motive or impelling reason for doing it." [38] To the best of my knowledge, Hutcheson never states the latter view explicitly and unequivocally. However, it is true, as we shall see, that his position does seem to imply this view.

But let us compare Frankena's views with those of Kydd. Frankena quotes from Hutcheson to show that according to the latter the term obligation has two meanings, the first being that according to which "I ought" entails "it is to my interest" and the second being that which refers us to the approbation of the moral sense. In this second sense to say that one is obliged is, according to Hutcheson, to mean that "every spectator, or he himself upon reflection, must approve his action, and disapprove his omitting it, if he considers fully all its circumstances." [39] Significantly, and in opposition to Kydd, Frankena says that the latter meaning of

---

[36] Kydd, *Reason and Conduct,* p. 38.
[37] *Ibid.,* p. 39.
[38] *Ibid.,* p. 23.
[39] Hutcheson, *Illustrations,* p. 232.

"ought" "has nothing directly to do with motivation." [40] In another passage from a different work Frankena discusses the view that moral judgments are expressions of some specifically moral attitude and adds "one would then regard this attitude as conative (unlike Hutcheson's moral sense), . . ." [41] Again, Frankena states clearly his interpretation of the moral sense as non-conative.

Arthur N. Prior finds Hutcheson ambiguous, Hume less so. He states that in Hume, less ambiguously than in Hutcheson, "justification is at bottom no more than a particular variety of excitement." [42]

Prior has maintained that "there is little or nothing in Hume's moral philosophy that cannot be traced to Hutcheson, but in Hume it is all more clear and pointed." [43] If this is indeed the case, it is interesting to find that there are the same curious difficulties in Hume's philosophy with respect to the relationship between justifying reasons and motivation. Consider, for example, the effect of putting next to each other two famous passages from Hume. The first begins with the following claim: "If morality had naturally no influence on human passions and actions, 'twere in vain to take such pains to inculcate it; . . ." [44] Later in this paragraph and in those paragraphs immediately following Hume goes on to insist that morals excite passions whereas reason does not. The second passage to which I wish to draw attention appears several sections later in the Treatise and reads as follows:

In short, it may be established as an undoubted maxim, *that no action can be virtuous, or morally good, unless there be in human nature some motive to produce it, distinct from the sense of its morality.*[45]

The first passage, then, proclaims that morality does influence action. In order to relate the issues involved to the framework of Hutcheson's theory, it is illuminating to rephrase the second passage in Hutcheson's terminology as follows: "No action can be virtuous, or morally good – the sort of action for which justifying reasons can be given – unless there be in human nature some exciting reason to produce it, distinct from the sense of its morality – and, hence, distinct from any motivation by justifying reasons."

The above passages in Hume together with the quotations we have considered from Kydd, Frankena, and Prior draw attention to some of

---

[40] Frankena, "Hutcheson's Moral Sense Theory," p. 364.
[41] Frankena, "Obligation and Motivation," p. 73.
[42] Arthur N. Prior, *Logic and the Basis of Ethics* (Oxford: Clarendon Press, 1949), p. 32.
[43] *Ibid.*, p. 31.
[44] Hume, *Treatise,* p. 457.
[45] *Ibid.*, p. 479.

the puzzles to be solved in attempting to discover the relationship of justifying reasons to motivation. In what follows it will be my contention (1) that Hutcheson, in his earlier works, was somewhat unclear concerning the role of the moral sense and the relationship between justification and "excitement"; (2) that he did formulate, as he went along, a position on these questions that was fairly consistent but untenable, and (3) that he seemed to be partly aware of the untenability of his position and, as a result, reformulated his moral sense doctrine in his later works such as the *System of Moral Philosophy*.

Let me proceed, therefore, by pointing to evidence for my contention that Hutcheson, in his earlier works, is ambiguous and unclear concerning the issues in question and therefore leaves himself open to the various interpretations which were noted above.

As we noted earlier, Hutcheson inherits from Shaftesbury a conviction that morality is not always the "path of greatest resistance," but is shot through with intrinsic appeal. With this conviction it is natural that Hutcheson should be persuaded that morality is intensely practical, dynamic, and moving. One expects him to hold some form of internalism according to which moral judgments would involve reference to conation. Curiously enough, however, Hutcheson does not devote much space in the *Inquiry* to discussing the influence of the moral sense on action. Having maintained that the motive from which we do virtuous actions consists in their being approved by the moral sense, he is confronted by a dilemma which he never completely resolves. If, on the one hand, benevolence is the motive from which virtuous acts are performed, then the moral sense, for all of its hedonistic attractions, is in danger of being superfluous as a source of motivation. However, since justifying reasons are said to presuppose the moral sense, this sense may serve as a source of justification. If, on the other hand, the moral sense is held to motivate, its pleasures giving rise to desires, then how, at the same time, can it serve to provide justification?

In the *Illustrations* Hutcheson seems to distinguish more clearly the difference between the exciting reasons which move to election, and the justifying reasons which move to approbation. He goes on to assert that there are cases in which justifying reasons do not motivate as, for example, in the case of approving actions of others which occurred in the distant past. He does not here discuss how justifying reasons do in fact motivate.[46]

As a means of clarifying Hutcheson's position, it is helpful to establish the place of benevolence in his theory. Throughout his entire theory, he

[46] Hutcheson, *Illustrations,* p. 248.

never wavers in maintaining that it is benevolence which is the immediate motive to virtuous actions and which is therefore approved by the moral sense. Possibly after falling under Butler's influence, Hutcheson, in later editions of the *Inquiry* and in the *Essay* and all works subsequent to it, maintains that the benevolence which is approved by the moral sense is not impulsive or "passionate" benevolence, but calm general benevolence. As discussed in a previous chapter, Hutcheson has appreciated a difference in kind between our violent impulses and the calm desires.

Is there such a motive as the calm general benevolence described by Hutcheson? Hume, on some occasions, denies this; Butler, although he does state that there is such a motive, is sometimes ambiguous. In his *Treatise,* Hume makes the following statement: "In general, it may be affirmed, that there is no such passion in human minds, as the love of mankind, merely as such, independent of personal qualities, of services, or of relation to ourself." [47] And Broad comments that Butler "sometimes tends to drop benevolence, as a general principle co-ordinate with self-love, rather out of sight, and to talk of it as if it were just one of the particular impulses." [48]

I think Hume's point is well-taken as having to do with man's original make-up. A native "passion" directed towards the good of others, would, even if it existed, be a rather shadowy and tenuous motive. Dewey and Tufts, when they consider the contribution to the general good as the end-in-view of desire, make the following statement:

It is hard to imagine its being made the end of desire; as a direct object to be aimed at, it would be so indeterminate and vague that it would only arouse a diffused sentimental state, without indicating just how and where conduct should be directed.[49]

Hutcheson, however, might well reply that calm benevolence is not an original appetite or "passionate desire." It is a desire which is directed by reason to the attainment of its objects. And just as self-love may be distinguished from our particular impulses directed towards objects such as food, drink, shelter, etc., so calm benevolence may be distinguished from the particular impulses which we have to seek the good of others.

It seems likely that there is at least one ambiguity in the term "benevolence" which Hutcheson fails to clarify. The term "benevolence" used as a noun may, according to its dictionary meaning, be used both to mean "an inclination to do good" and to mean "a kindly, charitable, activity."

[47] Hume, *Treatise,* p. 481.
[48] Broad, *Five Types of Ethical Theory,* p. 71.
[49] John Dewey and James H. Tufts, *Ethics* (rev. ed.; New York: Henry Holt and Company, 1936), p. 270.

In the first sense it refers to a motive; in the second, to an act which promotes good. It seems likely that Hutcheson believed two statements which are not at all identical. The first maintains that what the moral sense approves is benevolent motives. The second maintains that we ought to promote the good of others. The second is what Nowell-Smith calls the "duty of beneficence." [50] Further consideration of the "duty of beneficence" must be preceded by an examination of Hutcheson's theory of obligation. However, it may be suggested in advance that one of the perplexities facing Hutcheson is that if, as seems likely, he believes that what we ought to do is that which conforms to this "duty of beneficence" then the motive for so doing must be benevolence. But, if it is benevolence, what role can the moral sense have in influencing us to action?

Hutcheson has been accused by several commentators of confusing benevolence with the moral sense. Martineau says of Hutcheson that "after resolving, as we have seen, all virtue into benevolence, he identifies the Moral Sense with it, and reduces the distinction between them to a verbal illusion." [51] Raphael, in similar vein, claims that although approbation and benevolence are obviously different, "Hutcheson often tends to confuse them . . . or to regard the difference between them as if it were negligible." [52]

Close examination of Hutcheson fails to reveal any basis for the charges of Martineau and Raphael. Hutcheson seems to me to distinguish again and again between benevolence as a calm general desire which is approved by the moral sense and the moral sense itself. He maintains that one may be benevolent without having an consciousness of virtue. He states that general benevolence to mankind may exist even when we are not reflecting upon our own temper, nor delighted with the perception of our own virtue." [53] Benevolence may be the ground of virtue; it is in no sense the essence of it. Furthermore, Hutcheson takes pains to distinguish benevolence as a motive which is approved by the moral sense from the desire to obtain the pleasures issuing from the moral sense, a quite different motive.

The sort of perplexities reported by Martineau and Raphael have their real source in an area of Hutcheson's theory which has been curiously neglected. It has been rather widely assumed, I suspect, that the moral sense theory may have difficulties with justification, but that at least it provides for excitement. This assumption is unwarranted. Hutcheson

[50] Nowell-Smith, Ethics, p. 231.
[51] Martineau, Types of Ethical Theory, I, 558.
[52] Raphael, The Moral Sense, p. 22.
[53] Hutcheson, Essay, p. 6.

simply fails to give a clear and consistent account of how the moral sense and justifying reasons motivate.

The rather surprising observation must be made that throughout most of the *Inquiry*, during which Hutcheson restricts his discussion to moral goodness and moral virtue, it is apparent that no motivational part is played by the moral sense – at least not directly. The feeling of approval which has its source in the moral sense is subsequent to and logically distinct from the acts or character-dispositions in question. Hume makes this explicit as regards his own doctrine when he makes the following statement in the *Treatise*: "In short, it may be established as an undoubted maxim, *that no action can be virtuous, or morally good, unless there be in human nature some motive to produce it,* distinct from the sense of its morality." [54] Although Hutcheson's position on this score is stated less sharply and dramatically, it cannot be doubted that it is identical with that of Hume. Everywhere we find Hutcheson denouncing as false those theories which maintain that the motive to virtuous actions is self-love, pursuit of the pleasure which accompanies virtue, or indeed anything other than the "true spring" of virtuous actions, namely, benevolence. The consequences of this position are far-reaching. It clearly implies that the motive to virtuous or morally good actions can never be a sense of morality or duty. If this were the end of the matter, Hutcheson would have to admit that, as regards our moral motivation, the sense of virtue plays no part whatsoever. Human beings who were benevolent but who lacked a moral sense would have lost nothing affecting their moral motivation. Morality would at most add a sort of contemplative and speculative pleasure.

Hutcheson seems to shrink from these implications of his own doctrine. Hume seems to have detected this. In one of his letters to Hutcheson, Hume argues as follows: ". . . to every virtuous action there must be a motive or impelling passion distinct from virtue; . . . virtue can never be the sole motive to any action." [55] He then accuses Hutcheson of not assenting to this proposition. Hume's basis for this accusation may have its origin in some unpreserved letter from Hutcheson to Hume. His accusation may also have been occasioned either by Hutcheson's lack of clarity in tracing the consequences, which we noted above, of his doctrine, or by Hutcheson's later doctrine in which he makes the moral sense a faculty which has the power to govern and regulate our actions.

Let us attempt, therefore, to trace further the consequences of Hut-

[54] Hume, *Treatise,* p. 479.
[55] Greig, ed., *Hume's Letters,* I, 35.

cheson's view that the motive of virtuous actions is benevolence. What sort of account can he now give of the motivational function, if any, of the moral sense? How can he account for the existence of conscientious action and action from a sense of obligation or duty?

In order to follow Hutcheson's position as regards the motivational function of the moral sense, we will have to apply the results of the critical study of the concepts of "pleasure" and "desire" presented in Chapter I. The moral sense is a source of distinct kinds of pleasure and pain. No doubt a desire to emphasize their distinctness led Hutcheson, in revising his early editions of the *Inquiry*, to strike out, on many occasions, the term "pleasure" and substitute the term "approval" in writing of the "finer perceptions" which have their source in the moral sense. Yet, no matter how different approval may be from other pleasures in their raw feel as Hutcheson surveys them introspectively, approval still remains, like all pleasure, a kind of sensation. Consequently, approval as a kind of sensation is not an affection or passion or "spring of action."

Although approval is not itself a "spring of action," it is intimately related to desires which are "springs of action." Earlier, we distinguished the various contexts in which pleasures occur. There are, for example, the pleasures which follow the gratification of appetite or passion. In this context Hutcheson maintains that desire is directed towards objects, not towards pleasure. But many pleasures are not preceded by situations including the presence of passions and appetites. As Hutcheson says: "No man is distressed for want of fine smells, harmonious sounds, beautiful objects, wealth, power, or grandeur, previously to some opinion formed of these things as good, or some prior sensation of their pleasures." [56] Virtue is to be included in this list, for, as Hutcheson says, there is no appetite or passion towards virtue. But although there is no appetite toward virtue, there is a desire for virtue. In the *Essay* Hutcheson makes the following statement:

Desires arise in our mind, from the frame of our nature, upon apprehension of good or evil in objects, actions, or events, to obtain for ourselves or others the agreeable sensation, when the object or event is good; or to prevent the uneasy sensation when it is evil. [57]

He proceeds to divide desires into classes answering to the classes of our senses which are a source of pleasure and pain. One of these classes includes desires of virtue and aversion to vice.

In such passages as the above, Hutcheson seems, like any hedonist, to

[56] Hutcheson, *Essay*, p. 92.
[57] *Ibid.*, p. 7.

hold that desire is for pleasure. How can such passages be explained within his theory? In Chapter I it was concluded that Hutcheson's treatment of "desire" and "pleasure" is not entirely consistent. However, the context of his arguments is such as to suggest that he always returns at crucial points in his theory to the position that desire is directed towards objects, not towards pleasure, and that pleasure, although not an object of desire, may be a cause of desire. When he discusses the theory that virtue is pursued because of the concomitant pleasure he always objects that "this plainly supposes a sense of virtue antecedent to ideas of advantage, upon which this advantage is founded." [58] In other words, Hutcheson never makes the mistake of supposing that we can obtain the pleasures of virtue without acting virtuously any more than we can obtain the pleasures of chess without playing chess. Hutcheson would agree with Nowell-Smith that, as the latter says, "it is a logical truth that you cannot enjoy the pleasure of playing cricket without playing cricket." [59] However, Hutcheson would suppose that the question whether or not we experience some pleasure or other is an empirical question to be settled by an appeal to the data of reflection and sensation. And, as we mentioned earlier, it is on this score that he would be subject to some of the recent criticisms levelled against this sort of view by Ryle, Anscombe, Hampshire, and others.

In Chapter I I ascribed to Hutcheson the position that the desire aroused by the moral sense may be excited by pleasure, but does not have pleasure as its object. What, then, is its object? In the *System* Hutcheson gives this question its clearest answer. The desire for virtue or, as he prefers to call it in some chapters of the *System,* the "desire of moral excellence," must, he says, "presuppose some antecedent determinations of the will as its object." And, more specifically, among such determinations, it must presuppose "some one in which the supreme moral excellence consists." [60] This one determination is from first to last always identified by Hutcheson as "benevolence." And after he formulated his distinction between the calm and general determinations and the particular desires, he holds that that which is most approved is the most extensive calm benevolence.

We seem, therefore, to have arrived at a point where the moral sense is an influence upon conduct. Whereas benevolence is a virtuous motive in that it is approved by the moral sense, a further desire for virtue or

[58] Selby-Bigge, *British Moralists,* I, 92.
[59] Nowell-Smith, *Ethics,* p. 137.
[60] Hutcheson, *System,* I, 52.

moral excellence may have as its object the performance of actions motivated by calm general benevolence. It must surely be admitted that this is a highly complicated state of affairs! However, any critical evaluation of Hutcheson must take into account that this does not represent his entire position as regards moral motivation. In order to obtain a complete picture of his treatment of moral motivation it is necessary at this point to examine his theory of obligation and of the relationship of obligation to motivation.

OBLIGATION AND MOTIVATION

Rachael Kydd argues that whereas Samuel Clarke had emphasized moral propositions about rightness, Hutcheson believed that moral propositions are concerned, not with rightness, but with obligation.[61] To this it must surely be objected that Hutcheson is much preoccupied with the concepts of moral good, moral evil, virtue and vice, devoting very little space to the concept of obligation. Yet Kydd is correct in supposing that one of Hutcheson's underlying motives is to explain how morality is practical, an explanation which Clarke had failed to supply. Thus, in spite of the fact that Hutcheson devotes so much attention to moral appraisal and to the concepts of moral good, moral evil, virtue and vice, he is certainly interested in obligation and in providing an account of the reasons, both justifying and exciting, for our moral actions.

When he turned to give an account of moral obligation, we may suppose that Hutcheson proceeded as usual to look for the sources of this concept in sensation and reflection. Since his search yielded no new simple idea of obligation, he came to the conclusion that the meaning of "obligation" in the sense we should call "moral obligation" is such that it "includes the moral sense." [62] That is, he believes that a theory of obligation may be extracted from his moral sense doctrine. And, having this belief, he no doubt felt that his thoroughgoing discussions of the moral sense served as a background for his theory of obligation and made it unnecessary for him to devote a great deal of space and time to the latter.

Can a plausible theory of obligation be combined with or extracted from Hutcheson's moral sense theory? This question has interest and importance for Hutcheson's ethical theory. But, in addition, this question raises problems which one finds reappearing in related theories having to do with obligation and motivation. Most important, much of Hutche-

[61] Kydd, *Reason and Conduct,* p. 22.
[62] Hutcheson, *Illustrations,* p. 232.

son's account of obligation is adopted by Hume and forms a basis for continuing discussions of the latter's theory and of the relationships between "is" and "ought."

Hutcheson uses the term "obligation" in two senses. The one refers to what some eighteenth-century moralists called "interested obligation"; the other refers to what we should call "moral obligation." These two senses are identified in the following passage:

When we say one is obliged to an action, we either mean, 1. that the action is necessary to obtain happiness to the agent, or to avoid misery: Or, 2. that every spectator, or he himself upon reflection, must approve his action, and disapprove his omitting it, if he considers fully all its circumstances.[63]

In the *Inquiry* Hutcheson makes a distinction between "constraint" and "obligation." The former, "constraint," is equated with the first of the above uses of the term "obligation" in which it is connected with self-interest. He goes on to say: "when any sanctions co-operate with our moral sense, in exciting us to actions which we count morally good we say we are oblig'd; but when sanctions of rewards or punishments oppose our moral sense, then we say we are brib'd or constrain'd." [64] It is interesting to compare Hutcheson's terminology with that of Kant. The latter holds that all "ought" sentences are imperatives and involve the relation of "constraint" in that the will may be subject to conflicting determinations and may resist the dictates of the imperative.[65] By comparison, Hutcheson maintains that although what he sometimes calls "interested obligation" involves constraint, the sense of "ought" which we might call "moral obligation" involves no such constraint, being addressed to a will which is not depicted as in conflict, but as being in accord with the moral sense.

It should be noted that among those "interested obligations" which constrain us through self-interest is the obligation to approve and pursue virtue. In spite of the considerable differences between the theories of Butler, Hutcheson, and Hume, they share a very considerable interest in trying to convince the reader that virtuous action is to his advantage.

But leaving aside for the moment the role of "interested obligations," let us proceed to an examination of moral obligation and, in doing so, let us distinguish between the following questions: (1) What are we

---

[63] *Ibid.*, p. 232.
[64] Selby-Bigge, *British Moralists,* I, 159.
[65] Immanuel Kant, *Foundations of the Metaphysics of Morals* in *Immanuel Kant: Critique of Practical Reason and Other Writings in Moral Philosophy,* trans. and ed. by Lewis White Beck (Chicago: University of Chicago Press, 1949), p. 72.

THE MORAL SENSE AND MOTIVATION91

morally obliged to do? (2) From what motive do we do what we are morally obliged to do?

Beginning with the first of these questions, let us re-examine closely Hutcheson's statement that by "obligation" we mean, as he puts it, "that every spectator, or he himself upon reflection, must approve his action, and disapprove his omitting it, if he considers fully all its circumstances." [66] What we are obliged to do, therefore, is an act which is approved in commission, disapproved in omission. And in being obliged we experience disapproval. Certain ambiguities are inherent in Hutcheson's statement of this view. He could be taken to mean: (1) what we ought to do is to perform benevolent acts; (2) what we ought to do is to perform virtuous acts; or (3) we ought to perform certain acts which are approved in themselves, not because of their motives or the character-dispositions which give rise to them.

Let us try to discover which of these he maintains. In the *Inquiry* we find an early statement of his theory of obligation. He contrasts, as usual, two senses of the term "obligation." Of moral obligation he states:

If by obligation we understand a determination, without regard to our own interest, to approve actions, and to perform them; which determination shall also make us displeas'd with ourselves and uneasy upon having acted contrary to it; in this meaning of the word obligation, there is naturally an obligation upon all men to benevolence. . . .[67]

In this passage Hutcheson would appear to be saying that what we ought to do is to perform benevolent acts. This view is confronted with a formidable objection. If it is agreed that "ought" implies "can," and if it is agreed, further, that motives are not the sort of entities that can be summoned up at will, then it cannot be maintained that we have an obligation to act from benevolence or any other motive. It might be contended that we have an obligation to inculcate benevolence in ourselves and others, but that contention, if true, would be a different matter. Finally, as regards the view that what we ought to do is to perform benevolent actions, there is the curious consequence that the sense of obligation would then be inoperative as a motive. If we are obliged to act from benevolence, then, truistically, our motive cannot be anything but benevolence.

It is hard to understand how Hutcheson or anyone else could maintain the extremely implausible view that what we ought to do is to perform acts from a benevolent motive. That this view has some sort of continuing

[66] Hutcheson, *Illustrations,* p. 232.
[67] Selby-Bigge, *British Moralists,* I, 153.

appeal seems attested to by the fact that it continues to crop up in various theories. It seems plausible to suppose that a part of its appeal is caused by the fact that an inattentive reader switches back and forth, perhaps unconsciously, between two positions. According to the one, what we ought to do is to do good to others. Following Nowell-Smith's terminology, I shall refer to this in future as the "duty of beneficence." [68] According to the other, what we ought to do is to act from a benevolent motive. It seems very likely that Hutcheson is guilty of confusing these two positions.

In considering Hutcheson's doctrine of obligation, it was stated earlier that he could be taken to mean: (1) what we ought to do is to perform benevolent acts; (2) what we ought to do is to perform virtuous acts; or (3) we ought to perform certain acts which are approved in themselves, not because of their motives or the character-dispositions which give rise to them. Having criticized at length the first of these alternatives, let us turn to the second.

According to the second of the above alternatives, what we ought to do is to perform virtuous acts. This is the view which Prichard ascribes to Hutcheson.[69] Let us assume for the moment that this alternative does indeed represent Hutcheson's position. If what we ought to do is to perform virtuous actions, then from what motive would we perform them? The answer to this question returns us to that paradoxical state of affairs, already referred to, according to which the first and ultimate motive to virtuous actions can never be attributed to the moral sense or to a sense of obligation. As Hume puts it, *"no action can be virtuous or morally good, unless there be in human nature some motive to produce it, distinct from the sense of its morality."* [70] There is no doubt that Hutcheson subscribes to the latter statement. Set in the form of an argument, his position might be set forth as follows: "What we ought to do is to perform virtuous actions. And a virtuous action must have as its motive some 'antecedent determination' which, as a matter of fact, is calm benevolence. The conclusion follows that when we do what we ought our motive must be benevolence." It follows, also, that our motive in doing what we ought can never be a sense of obligation or the approval of the moral sense. Prichard, in ascribing a nearly identical argument to Hume, states that such an argument proves that the motive for doing what we ought "can *never* be the sense of duty." [71]

[68] Nowell-Smith, *Ethics*, p. 231.
[69] Prichard, *Moral Obligation*, p. 152.
[70] Hume, *Treatise*, p. 479.
[71] Prichard, *Moral Obligation*, p. 157.

Two comments may be added with reference to Hutcheson's position. In the first place, if what we ought to do is acts motivated by benevolence, then we must object that this position has already been examined and found wanting. In the second place, if both what we ought to do and virtuous acts can only be motivated by benevolence, then the moral sense would seem to be left without any motivational function whatsoever, a curious consequence if one believes that one of Hutcheson's underlying purposes was to show how morality is dynamic and how moral judgments move to action.

But, let us recall that, earlier in this chapter, we did discover how the moral sense might motivate. It was concluded that whereas benevolence is the motive approved by the moral sense, the approval of the moral sense may in turn give rise to a desire whose object is the performance of benevolent acts. This being the case, might we not suppose that the motive for doing what we ought is not benevolence, but a desire to act virtuously? This desire would be coextensive with what Hutcheson refers to in the *System* as the desire for moral excellence.

In distinguishing between a desire for virtue and a virtuous motive Hutcheson is making a distinction in which he is followed by Hume. Writing of the latter, Aiken states:

Hume is here distinguishing between a moral or virtuous motive and a motive whose purpose is "a regard for virtue." This is not a quibble. A virtuous motive is, briefly, a benevolent motive. A regard for virtue is a regard either for the *approval* of a virtuous or moral person or for the maxims which such a person would approve. The latter is what we call "the sense of duty" or, perhaps, "conscience." [72]

Aiken's comments may be applied equally to Hutcheson. It should be emphasized, therefore, that the only way in which the moral sense or a sense of obligation may move us is through the desire whose object is the performance of virtuous acts.

But now it is crucial that we attend to the full force and the implications of the above view which Aiken attributes to Hume and which we have traced to Hutcheson. The more closely this view is examined the more it seems to generate puzzles and paradoxes.[73] The first of these is

[72] Henry D. Aiken, ed., *Hume's Moral and Political Philosophy* (New York: Hafner Publishing Company, 1948), p. xxxv.

[73] Apart from the fact that they have a classic source in the theories of Hutcheson and Hume, some of these puzzles have their counterpart in other contexts. I am indebted, for example, to John Ladd's penetrating discussion of the paradoxes which arise if one supposes that there is a desire to do one's duty for its own sake. [John Ladd, "The Desire to Do One's Duty for Its Own Sake" in *Morality and the Language of Conduct,* ed. by Hector-Neri Castaneda and George Nakhnikian (Detroit: Wayne State University Press, 1963).]

what I shall dub the "double-desire paradox." Consider the following as an example of the sort of motivation which would be required by Hutcheson's theory. Let us suppose that I, a violinist, have promised a dying friend that on a certain future date I will perform his favorite sonata, Beethoven's *Spring Sonata,* and that I will play it, as nearly as possible, in the manner in which it was performed by his favorite violinist, Bronislaw Hubermann. Let us further suppose that such a request is one which I have the knowledge and skill to fulfill. Presumably, when Hubermann once played this work he had certain artistic motives, intentions and/or causes of his performance. If I now perform this sonata out of a sense of duty I must do so from two motives: (1) a desire to do my duty; (2) the sort of desires which motivated Hubermann in the first place – discounting the possibility that without such desires one could produce a close imitation of his performance of such a lengthy work. The question arises: which desire is operative or are both? If both, can I be said to be acting out of a sense of duty if, halfway through, I completely forget myself, and play from the sort of motives which Hubermann had, rather than from a sense of duty? But, on the other hand, since my duty is to play like Hubermann, how can I fulfill this duty without acting from the sort of motives that Hubermann had?

Let us compare this sort of predicament with the position we have been ascribing to Hutcheson according to which the motive for doing what we ought is a desire to act virtuously. Again, in his terminology, a desire to act virtuously is a desire to do what is approved. In turn, this approval is always occasioned by the presence of a benevolent motive. In cases of doing what we ought, we should therefore witness the operation of a sort of "double-desire" or "double-motive." That is, to act out of a desire for virtue, one would have to act out of a desire to act from a second desire. Paradoxically, I cannot act out of a sense of obligation unless I am already motivated by benevolence, and if I am already motivated by benevolence what need is there for a desire to be motivated by benevolence? Apart from the air of paradox surrounding this position one wonders nightmarishly if there might be further conjunctions taking the form of desires-to-desire-to-desire.

In defending Hutcheson, someone might frame the following reply to the above observations: "Granted that we cannot act out of a desire to be motivated by benevolence when the latter motive is actually present, we may nevertheless be motivated by a desire to be benevolent when we find ourselves lacking in the motive of benevolence." Hutcheson simply does not discuss this sort of point. It is plausible to suppose that he may

not have attached much moral significance or worth to our being motivated by a desire to be benevolent when we find ourselves lacking in the
motive of benevolence. This might be inferred from some of the arguments which he presented in the course of his refutation of egoism. These
arguments, which have already been treated at length, sought to establish
that no act of volition could raise a desire in us. Furthermore, he maintained, self-love may raise a desire-for-a-desire for the happiness of others,
but it cannot simply raise a desire for the happiness of others. It may be,
therefore, that Hutcheson would consider that a desire to be benevolent
when we are lacking in benevolence could only be raised by self-love or
some motive which is of no moral worth.

It is illuminating to compare Hutcheson's position in these respects
with that of Hume. Consider again the claim set forth above: "Granted
that we cannot act out of a desire to be motivated by benevolence when
the latter motive is actually present, we may nevertheless be motivated
by a desire to be benevolent when we find ourselves lacking in the motive
of benevolence." This would seem to be the very point Hume has in mind
when he describes the operation of "a certain sense of duty" which may
motivate even in the absence of virtuous motives. He makes the following
statement:

When any virtuous motive or principle is common in human nature, a person,
who feels his heart devoid of that motive, may hate himself upon that account, and may perform the action without the motive, from a certain sense
of duty, in order to acquire by practice, that virtuous principle, or at least, to
disguise to himself as much as possible his want of it.[74]

The agent is advised, like Hamlet's mother, to "assume a virtue if you
have it not."

Upon examination, it would appear that Hume's "certain sense of
duty" cannot avoid the objections raised above against conceiving of the
sense of duty as a desire-to-desire. The trouble is that Hume's "certain
sense of duty" is parasitic in the sense that, in spite of his claims to the
contrary, it cannot operate in the absence of virtuous motives, but must
depend upon them for a more full-blooded moral motivation. Cartoon
editors, in evaluating cartoons submitted to them, may go about their
grading humorlessly, making mechanical applications of certain criteria.
But these criteria must be related ultimately to a sense of humor. Similarly, an agent may sometimes lack the primary moral motivation approved
as virtuous and may in such cases try to act as if he had it. But if he
continues without relationship to the more primary and full-blooded

[74] Hume, *Treatise*, p. 479.

motivation, then the parasitic desire to act virtuously must degenerate into hypocrisy. It is no doubt this aspect of Hume's position which T. H. Green has in mind when he points out that this doctrine explains only " 'respectability' the temper of the man who 'naturally,' i.e. without definite expectation of ulterior gain, seeks to stand well with his neighbors. . . ." [75]

In summary, let us retrace the preceding arguments. On the one hand, when benevolence motivates and is approved, we cannot at the same time be motivated by the *desire* to be benevolent, for this desire is consequent upon our approval. On the other hand, when we find ourselves lacking in benevolence, our desire to obtain approval may indeed motivate. However, the latter sort of motivation is seen to be parasitic in the sense that it would degenerate into hypocrisy if the agent were lacking in all of that primary motivation which is originally approved. We may conclude, therefore, that the moral sense and the sense of obligation which, in Hutcheson's opinion, presupposes the moral sense, cannot motivate at all except in a very restricted and parasitic sense.

Related to the "double-desire paradox" is the paradox of what might be called the "vanishing moral motive." This paradox appears whenever it is held that under ideal circumstances a good man will always act from such natural motives as benevolence rather than from a sense of duty or from any moral consideration whatsoever. Nowell-Smith seems to be maintaining this view in the following passage:

> The sense of duty is a useful device for helping men to do what a really good man would do without a sense of duty; and since none of us belongs to the class of "really good men" in this sense, it is a motive that should be fostered in all of us. But it plays little part in the lives of the best men and could play none at all in the lives of saints.[76]

On Hutcheson's view, is it not conceivable that a man might be called virtuous by his friends and yet have no moral sense or sense of obligation whatsoever? It is true that whenever we judge acts to be morally good or virtuous such judgments presuppose, for Hutcheson, the existence of a moral sense. But the moral sense presupposed is that of persons making such judgments and thereby expressing their approval. Granting this, why are the acts or character-dispositions approved dependent on a moral sense? In calling an agent or his acts virtuous and thereby expressing our approval of them need we suppose that the agent *himself* is aware of his

[75] Green, "Introduction to the Moral Part of Hume's 'Treatise,' " in *Works of Thomas Hill Green,* I, 370.

[76] Nowell-Smith, *Ethics,* p. 259.

own virtue, i.e. need we suppose that he approves of himself? Hutcheson, following Shaftesbury, would no doubt answer in the negative. As Hutcheson says:

... many are strongly affected with the fortunes of others, who seldom reflect upon virtue or vice, in themselves, or others, as an object: as we may find in natural affection, compassion, friendship, or even general benevolence to mankind, which connects our happiness or pleasure with that of others, even when we are not reflecting upon our own temper, nor delighted with the perception of our own virtue.[77]

In short, we must not suppose that Hutcheson equates virtue with benevolence. A character-disposition or act is virtuous if it is approved upon reflection; benevolence is that motive which is, as a matter of fact, approved. A man might be benevolent without being aware of being virtuous.

But in this case we encounter an instance of the "vanishing moral motive." That is, if a man might act entirely from benevolence without being aware of his own goodness, then it follows, curiously enough, that neither the moral sense nor moral judgments play any part in the motivation of such a man. If Hutcheson then were to maintain, like Nowell-Smith, that since none of us is ideally good the desire for virtue aroused by the moral sense is needed to inculcate benevolence, then we may return to our comments concerning the limited and "parasitic" nature of this desire for virtue.

Let us continue tracing those characteristics of Hutcheson's doctrine of obligation and motivation which, taken together, render it wholly untenable. Joseph Butler had included in his theory an appeal to the authoritative character of conscience. Hutcheson's earlier theory does not follow Butler in this respect. His later theory, following the *Illustrations*, does. Let us suppose that Butler and other more recent writers such as John Ladd [78] and Bernard Mayo [79] are correct in maintaining that moral judgments are somehow authoritative and overriding. How can Hutcheson's earlier theory do justice to this position?

Consider the following example. I find a wallet containing a considerable sum of money, together with cards identifying its owner. Upon deliberating as to what to do, I find that I am aware of two desires, the one prompting me to keep the money, the other prompting me to return

[77] Hutcheson, *Essay*, p. 6.
[78] John Ladd, *The Structure of a Moral Code* (Cambridge, Mass.: Harvard University Press, 1957), p. 79.
[79] Bernard Mayo, *Ethics and the Moral Life* (London: Macmillan & Co., 1958), p. 160.

it to its owner, even though I am confident I should never be discovered if I did not return it. My personal need for the money, furthermore, may be very great and the owner may be the sort of man who would hardly miss it.

What would Hutcheson say of such a example? Certainly that I ought to return the money. This "ought" clearly serves to provide justification. Let us not pause to renew the quarrel with Hutcheson's notion of justification as residing in the approval of the moral sense. Instead let us ask how the judgment that I ought to return the money is related to motivation. Presumably, as traced earlier in great detail, approval of that benevolent motive which prompts me to return the money gives rise to a desire to do as I ought and if I were to act upon the latter desire I should then come to feel a satisfaction in having done so. But why, in a motivational sense, should this desire dominate or be preferred to my desire for keeping the money? Hutcheson may reply that I will be happier if I do as I ought. He argues again and again that the pleasures of virtuous actions will exceed those of vicious or evil actions. But even if he is right in this contention, it may be doubted that he intends this as an answer to the question as to why I should be moved by a desire to do my duty and return the money rather than by a desire to keep it for myself. In view of his careful distinctions between the motives prompting us to perform our "interested obligations" and the disinterested motives prompting us to perform virtuous actions, it seems incredible to suppose that the desire to do my duty might be overriding merely because of its contribution to self-love.

A related issue which needs to be considered concerns Hutcheson's account of the contingent character of the desire to do as we ought. Hutcheson is indeed concerned to show that moral judgments influence action. Strictly speaking, however, his theory must be counted as a kind of "externalism." As we indicated earlier, moral judgments, for Hutcheson, may be interpreted either as expressive of or as stating the existence of a peculiar kind of pleasurable reaction. According to Hutcheson, pleasure is a kind of sensation, not a motive, although it may give rise to desires which *are* motives. Thus the relationships between moral judgments and conation must be causal, as in the case of "externalist" theories, not logical, as in the case of "internalist" theories. The desire aroused by the pleasure of the moral sense is contingent, not necessary. It is simply a matter of fact that human beings sometimes do have benevolent motives and sometimes are motivated by a desire to do right actions, a desire aroused by a feeling of approval which is also contingent, not necessary.

But the strict internalist may object at this point that motivation is logically tied to obligation. He may claim, as Ladd does, that when the desire to do one's duty for its own sake is taken to be an empirically observable desire, then "this desire – unlike ordinary desires, which are contingent – would appear to be, in some sense, necessary." [80] Our ordinary discourse contains many expressions which do not fit readily into an account which holds to the contingent character of our motivation to do what we ought. Consider the example of the orchestral conductor who says "You ought to play *staccato* in bar 128" and is told in reply, "Sorry, I agree with your judgment, but at the moment I just don't have any desire to play the way I ought to." Or, in a moral context, consider the comment "I grant that I ought to do x, but of course I won't do it because I have no motive whatsoever." Internalists will insist that there is an air of logical impropriety in such examples.

In locating Hutcheson's position with respect to these issues, we may discount two extreme positions as regards the problem of the relationship between obligation and motivation. At the one extreme, it might be maintained that a strict logical entailment holds between the statement "I ought to do x" and the statement "I have a motive for performing x." But upon examination this will not do. As Broad puts it: "So far as I can see there would not be the slightest inconsistency in supposing that a being who was rational in the ethically neutral sense, and did in fact have the ideas of right and wrong and make moral judgments, was completely devoid of specifically moral emotion and conation." [81] Samuel Clarke is typical of those rationalists, opposed by Hutcheson, who simply assume without further explanation an extremely close connection between obligation and motivation. At the other extreme, Broad's statement indicates the possibility of maintaining that not only is there no logical connection between obligation and motivation, but that there is only a weak causal connection between them. Hutcheson's position falls between these extremes. The desire which follows approval by the moral sense is contingent, but the connection between this desire and approval is a close as it may be in the realm of matters of fact.

In answer to the charge that the desire to do as one ought is necessary, not contingent, Hutcheson could only point out that although the connection between obligation and motivation can only be contingent, human nature is such that we do as a matter of fact desire what is ap-

[80] Ladd, "The Desire To Do One's Duty," p. 323.
[81] Broad, "Moral-Sense Theories in Ethics," p. 384.
[82] Hutcheson, *Illustrations*, p. 245.

proved by the moral sense. The internalist, however, may comment that the closeness of the connection between obligation and motivation in Hutcheson leads one to suspect that the terms "desire" and "pleasure" are not as empirically grounded as Hutcheson would have us believe.

A comment should be made, however, concerning the fact that Hutcheson was himself troubled by the contingent character of our moral sense and our moral motivation. This led him to a theological move, maintaining that our instincts are not arbitrary, but are such as to be themselves approved by God. Hutcheson asks: "Why may not the Deity have something of a superior kind, analogous to our moral sense, essential to him?" [82] Earlier, in the *Inquiry*, Hutcheson had presented an argument which Prior has referred to as the "argument from trivialization." [83] This appears in Hutcheson as follows: ". . . to call the laws of the supreme Deity good, or holy, or just, if all goodness, holiness and justice be constituted by laws, or by the will of a superior any way revealed, must be an insignificant tautology, amounting to no more than this 'That God wills what he wills.' " [84] Hutcheson's rationalist opponent Balguy saw that the latter sort of argument might be employed against Hutcheson's own theological move which tries to escape the arbitrariness of our instincts and moral sense. As Balguy points out, may we not ask concerning a Deity who is said to have a moral sense: "Is such a disposition a perfection in the Deity or is it not?" [85] Has not Hutcheson simply said, to use his own phrase, that God wills what he wills, approves what he approves, etc. And can we not, as Balguy suggests, go on to ask meaningfully the question "But is what God's moral sense approves really good?" [86]

Having considered some of the difficulties arising from Hutcheson's position regarding obligation and its relationship to motivation, we must return to an examination of the last of the three views which were listed as being open to Hutcheson in answer to the question "What ought we to do?" Again, these views are: (1) what we ought to do is to perform benevolent actions; (2) what we ought to do is to perform virtuous actions; or (3) we ought to perform certain actions which are approved in themselves, not because of their motives or the character-dispositions which give rise to them. The first and second views have in common that what is approved is not actions as such, but the motives and character-dispositions giving rise to them. The third view, in maintaining that what

[83] Prior, *Logic and the Basis of Ethics,* p. 110.
[84] Selby-Bigge, *British Moralists,* I, 158.
[85] John Balguy, *The Foundation of Moral Goodness,* in Selby-Bigge, *British Moralists,* II, 61.
[86] *Ibid.*

we approve and ought to perform are actions, would appear to be a much simpler view. Prichard, for example, argues as follows:

... the rightness of an action concerns an action not in the fuller sense of the term in which we include the motive in the action, but in the narrower and commoner sense in which we distinguish an action from its motive and mean by an action merely the conscious origination of something, an origination which on different occasions or in different people may be prompted by different motives.[87]

The question arises, therefore, as to whether or not Hutcheson could be interpreted as holding that (1) we approve, not only of character-dispositions and motives, but of actions; (2) we are obliged to perform actions, not to have certain motives; (3) our motive in doing what we ought is a desire aroused by our approval or disapproval of actions. Rachael Kydd defends this interpretation of Hume, whose theory is in these respects much like that of Hutcheson.[88]

Let us turn to Hutcheson with this interpretation in mind. At first glance, phrases do appear in which he speaks of "approving actions." Even in his definition of "obligation" it is actions which are said to be approved. By "obligation" in the sense of "moral obligation" he claims that we mean "that every spectator, or he himself upon reflection, must approve his action, and disapprove his omitting it, if he considers fully all its circumstances." [89] But if we look more closely at the context of this and similar statements, we find that what Hutcheson really means is that what we approve is not the action *per se,* but the action as evidence of a certain motive or character-disposition. If Hutcheson were willing to adopt the view that what we ought to do is *acts,* rather than acts performed from a certain motive, then the sense of obligation would differ from the moral sense, for the latter is always taken by Hutcheson to approve previous "natural determinations" or motives. But he states repeatedly that the meaning of obligation, as he puts it, "includes the moral sense." [90] Hence we may infer that obligation is linked to virtue, moral goodness, and the moral sense in such a way that it is utterly implausible to ascribe to Hutcheson the view that we approve of acts apart from their motives. His view is quite consistent. We approve only of actions which spring from our affections. The moral sense must have as its object "antecedent determinations of the will."

In summary, therefore, it may be observed that some of the difficulties

[87] Prichard, *Moral Obligation,* p. 6.
[88] Kydd, *Reason and Conduct,* p. 192.
[89] Hutcheson, *Illustrations,* p. 232.
[90] *Ibid.*

of Hutcheson's position might have been avoided if he had held the view that what we approve and ought to perform are *actions,* not actions from certain motives, a view which Kydd ascribes to Hume. However, from our examination of Hutcheson we must conclude that this view cannot be ascribed to him. In passing, it might be remarked that similar considerations render doubtful Kydd's interpretation of Hume.

CONCLUDING REMARKS

Let us attempt to draw together some of the conclusions of this chapter. At the very beginning of this chapter Rachael Kydd was quoted as saying: "Hutcheson made it clear that judgments which verify moral propositions must also be capable of influencing us to action, but his analysis of these judgments remained obscure." [91] Prior and Frankena were seen to be in disagreement, the former maintaining that justification is, for Hutcheson, a kind of excitement, the latter maintaining that the moral sense is non-conative. Our critical examination of Hutcheson has attempted to clarify Hutcheson's doctrines as regards the way in which moral judgments influence to action. Briefly, his position is that "justification" and "excitement" are to be distinguished, but that justification, somewhat indirectly, may excite to action. This occurs when the moral sense, on which all justifying reasons must depend, provides us with unique pleasures or pains which in turn may arouse desire. Thus, although, strictly speaking, Frankena is correct in describing the moral sense as "non-conative," this sense is nevertheless causally related to conation.

When we traced in detail the answer to the question how the moral sense or the sense of obligation actually motivate, we found, on repeated occasions, the following predicament: either the moral sense and the sense of obligation were not the source of our moral motivation or else, when they did in fact motivate, Hutcheson's account of how this occurred was full of difficulties.

In summary, let us recall Hutcheson's position relative to the controversy between the "externalists" and "internalists" concerning the relationship of obligation to motivation. His position is not easily classified. He maintains that the approval of the moral sense as a matter of fact gives rise to desire. And, as we claimed earlier, he is certainly an externalist in maintaining that the motivation to which the moral sense gives rise is not logically entailed by moral judgments.

[91] Kydd, *Reason and Conduct,* p. 39.

Yet there is an air of internalism clinging to Hutcheson's theory. In part at least, this may be traceable to the status of a proposition which may be stated as follows: "All expressions of approval are preceded by certain 'natural determinations' or motives." Hutcheson of course maintains the truth of this proposition. Is it a logical truth? Or can it be meaningfully contradicted? Since, according to Hutcheson, approval is a peculiar kind of pleasure, it is hard to see why it should be logically tied to objects and why, therefore, the proposition in question should not be capable of being contradicted. Quite apart from Hutcheson, the logic of sentences containing the term "approval" seems to be such that "approval" is always, logically speaking, of objects. It seems likely, therefore, that Hutcheson's theory benefits from the ambiguities surrounding the term "approval" and comes to suggest that the proposition "all expressions of approval are preceded by certain 'natural determinations' or motives" is a logical truth. If this were indeed the case, moral judgments would always imply the presence of motivation. It must be strongly emphasized, however, that the motivation implied would not be in any way dependent upon the moral sense, being antecedent to its operation. The foregoing remarks may serve in part to explain how Hutcheson's theory has the appearance of being "internalist" whereas, strictly, speaking, it must be classified as "externalist."

One rather simple point needs to be given emphasis, namely, that through the conception of a moral sense which is both a source of justification and of excitement, Hutcheson hoped to find an answer, not only to Clarke and the egoists, but to all moralists who had ever pondered on the relation of "is" to "ought." The pivotal character of this conception was not lost on David Hume. Commentators who search for a way to close "Hume's gap," the gap between "is" and "ought," would do well to ponder what he refers to as a "new fact" in the following statement:

Morals and criticism are not so properly objects of the understanding as of taste and sentiment. Beauty, whether moral or natural, is felt, more properly than perceived. Or if we reason concerning it, and endeavor to fix its standard, we regard a new fact, to wit, the general tastes of mankind, or some such fact, which may be the object of reasoning and enquiry.[92]

And, as a matter of fact, Philippa Foot does contend that it is through the sentiment of approbation that Hume bridges the gap between "is" and "ought" and establishes a necessary connection between morality and the will. She goes on to maintain that

[92] Hume, *Enquiry Concerning Human Understanding*, p. 165.

... the moral sentiment, the special feeling which we call approbation, was a pleasurable sentiment, by which we were inclined towards those actions whose contemplation gave rise to it. "To know virtue is to love it." This, Hume might have said, is a logical truth.[93]

Since Hume and Hutcheson are in essential agreement concerning their employment of the sentiment of approbation, we may examine how Foot's interpretation of these issues relates to Hutcheson. If her interpretation of Hume were applied to Hutcheson, it would follow that he must be a strict internalist. To this type of theory Foot raises the objection that it insists "on too close a connexion between moral judgment and the will." [94] And, indeed, one might go on to wonder at the sort of "instant motivation" which moral judgments would provide on such a view. This view cannot allow that any "gap" or "lag" might exist between a person's becoming enlightened in his moral views and his having an equal enlightenment in his motivation.

However, we need not pursue at greater length the objections against the sort of theory which Foot ascribes to Hume since it seems not at all likely that Hutcheson held it. He criticizes severely those who maintain that "the same reasons determining approbation, ought also to excite to election," going on to argue that "we often see justifying reasons where we can have no election, viz. when we observe the actions of others, which were even prior to our existence." [95] To be sure, he is here discussing justifying reasons, not moral judgments. However, his comments do cast doubt on any claim that the approbation expressed by moral judgments is necessarily practical and motivational.

Even more important for the evaluation of Foot's comments on the sort of theory we have been considering is the precise nature of Hutcheson's treatment of approval and its relationship to desire. On the sort of theory she ascribes to Hume and which we are considering with respect to Hutcheson, "to know virtue is to love it." And this, she adds, might have been said to be a logical truth. However it is not at all clear that Hutcheson would have agreed. He might have agreed that "to know virtue is to *approve* it" and that this is indeed a logical truth. But, strictly speaking, approval is not to be equated with love. On Hutcheson's theory, human nature is such that we do as a matter of fact love or desire what is approved. He presents this as an empirical theory. Hence the connection between moral judgments which express approval and motivation

[93] Foot, "Hume on Moral Judgment," p. 74.
[94] *Ibid.*, p. 75.
[95] Hutcheson, *Illustrations,* p. 248.

must be contingent, not necessary. The internalist may now be expected to comment that the extreme closeness of the connection between moral judgments and motivation in Hutcheson leads one to suspect that the terms "desire" and "pleasure" are not as empirically grounded as Hutcheson would have us believe. At various points in our discussion, we have expressed agreement with this sort of comment. It is precisely this sort of worry concerning empiricist accounts of pleasure, desire, and motivation in general that has inspired the reexamination of these issues by contemporary writers such as Ryle, Hampshire, and Anscombe.

In conclusion, we may note some curious consequences following from our comparison of Hutcheson with the early rationalists as regards the controversy between internalism and externalism. Frankena finds in intuitionism "the most striking example" of externalism.[96] If we may regard the rationalists as also maintaining a form of intuitionism, then we recall that, as we discussed in detail, they tended like Price to hold to an inseparable connection between obligation and motivation. They are therefore, contrary to Frankena, inclined towards a form of internalism, granted that their internalism is often rather dogmatic and uncritical. Hutcheson, on the other hand, whose theory has an air of internalism, turns out, on close inspection, to be a kind of externalist. And, against those who have supposed that Hutcheson can account for excitement but not for justification, I have contended that he has difficulties with both.

[96] Frankena, "Obligation and Motivation," p. 43.

CHAPTER IV

MOTIVATION AND THE MORAL SENSE IN HUTCHESON'S LATER WORKS

In the last chapter we found that when Hutcheson's theory of motivation is combined with his moral sense doctrine, the result is the appearance of paradoxes, puzzles, and, in general, an inadequate account of how moral judgments influence action. The examination of Hutcheson thus far has been directed mainly to three works, namely, the *Inquiry,* the *Essay,* and the *Illustrations.* Since these are the works which had most historical influence, it seems reasonable that they should be emphasized in any study of Hutcheson.

However, Hutcheson's later works are of considerable interest for our study because of the fact that they show evidence that he was aware of and made attempts to remedy some of the very deficiencies in his earlier position to which we have devoted attention. The later works with which we shall be mostly concerned are the *Short Introduction to Moral Philosophy* and the *System of Moral Philosophy.* Little of added interest is to be found in the *Metaphysicae Synopsis Ontologiam et Pneumatologiam complectens,* the only other work of any magnitude written after the *Illustrations.* Comments on Hutcheson's later doctrine will be restricted to those aspects of it which have to do with our main topic, the moral sense and how it relates to motivation.

The most noteworthy differences between Hutcheson's earlier and later positions have to do with alterations in his description of the nature and function of the moral sense. In his later works the moral sense is still described as the source of a peculiar kind of pleasure, but, in addition, it is now referred to by various other terms. In the *Short Introduction to Moral Philosophy,* the moral sense is often referred to by the term "conscience" and is described as serving to "regulate the highest powers of our nature." [1] In the *System,* the moral sense is sometimes referred to

---

[1] Hutcheson, *Short Introduction,* p. 16.

as the "faculty of perceiving moral excellence" [2] and in this work Hutcheson maintains the following:

This moral sense from its very nature appears to be designed for regulating and controlling all our powers. This dignity and commanding nature we are immediately conscious of, as we are conscious of the power itself.[3]

In such passages as the above, the influence of Butler's doctrine of conscience and of his claim that conscience has a distinctive authority is clearly evident, although it should be remarked that Hutcheson, like Butler himself, was often preoccupied with the origin of this doctrine in the Stoics.

Looking more closely into these changes in Hutcheson's position we find that his references to a "faculty of perceiving moral excellence" are in a context which suggests that virtue is a quality. In some passages this is rendered explicit. For example, he maintains at one point the following:

... when we admire the virtue of another, the whole excellence, or that quality which by nature we are determined to approve, is conceived to be in that other; we are pleased in the contemplation because the object is excellent, and the object is not judged to be therefore excellent because it gives us pleasure.[4]

In Chapter II we presented in detail arguments to the effect that this sort of passage simply cannot be rendered consistent with earlier views according to which to perceive moral excellence is symply to feel approval. Now we might hope that Hutcheson would follow up the above passage with a precise and sustained analysis which would clarify his position. But no such analysis is forthcoming. Hence we are left with indications of a naively realistic theory of the moral sense which, as we maintained earlier, is nevertheless entirely foreign to his general epistemological outlook.

Hutcheson's position is equally troublesome as regards the "Butlerian" characteristics now ascribed to the moral sense. In a letter following his reception of Hutcheson's *Short Introduction*, Hume addresses Hutcheson as follows:

You seem here to embrace Dr. Butler's opinion in his Sermons on Human Nature; that our moral sense has an authority distinct from its force and durableness, and that because we always think it *ought* to prevail. But this is nothing, but an instinct or principle, which approves of itself upon reflection; and that is common to all of them.[5]

---

[2] Hutcheson, *System*, I, 53.
[3] *Ibid.*, I, 61.
[4] *Ibid.*, I, 54.
[5] Greig, ed., *Letters of Hume*, I, 47.

But what does Hume mean by the last sentence of this quotation? Does he really intend to claim that all instincts or principles approve of themselves upon reflection? Raphael assumes that Hume must be referring either "to the fact that every desire 'clamors' as we say, for satisfaction" or "to the fact that we are prone to try to justify to ourselves many of our desires." [6] But this interpretation cannot account for the fact that even on Hume's theory there is a manifest difference between those desires and principles which operate without the approval of the moral sense and those which receive this approval.

Let us consider another possibility. The above quotation is, after all, from a letter, and Hume may have expressed himself carelessly. With this thought in mind, might it not be possible that the word "that" in the last sentence was intended to refer to or connect with the phrase "we always think it *ought* to prevail." If this were the case, Hume might be interpreted as affirming something like the following: "It is common to all instincts or principles which are approved upon reflection that we always think they ought to prevail." This interpretation saves Hume from inconsistency, but presupposes that he expressed himself very badly on this occasion.

Regardless of how certain phrases in Hume's letter are to be interpreted, we may nevertheless follow the general direction which his argument against Hutcheson might take with respect to the latter's ascription of authority to the moral sense. According to Hume's theory and, indeed, according to the theory Hutcheson held in his earlier works, the terms "authoritative" and "regulative" cannot possible be used to describe the moral sense. We need only recall the outlines of what has been argued earlier in detail. The moral sense, like any sense, is for Hutcheson a passive source of ideas. However, the feelings of approval and disapproval which originate in this sense may give rise to desires and aversions. Justifying reasons have their source in feelings of approval or disapproval; these reasons presuppose the existence of the moral sense. Hence justification is related to motivation through the fact that approbation may arouse desire. But how can these characteristics of the moral sense be consistent with ascribing authority to it? The answer is simply that they cannot. As a consequence, we find Hume denying the authorititative character of conscience and retaining a view which has much in common with Hutcheson's earlier theory.

But in the last chapter we concluded that Hutcheson's earlier theory led to errors, puzzles, and paradoxes when he tried to show how the moral

---

[6] Raphael, *The Moral Sense*, p. 93.

sense is related to motivation. It seems plausible to suppose that the changes which Hutcheson made in his later theory resulted from his awareness of difficulties and inadequacies in his earlier theory. One such change was his ascription of authority to the moral sense, a change which he no doubt felt would better express the relation between moral principles and moral action. Those who feel that the moral life exhibits an organization and that moral principles are not merely approved, but overriding, authoritative, or regulative will side with Hutcheson against Hume in the former's struggles to find a place for these convictions within his theory. And, on this score, I should be inclined to join them.

But, although Hutcheson's struggles to amend his earlier theory are commendable in themselves, the results are not philosophically satisfying. He makes little attempt to reconcile his earlier doctrine of the moral sense with his later doctrine according to which this sense is given new functions. One cannot tell whether he was simply blissfully unaware of the inconsistencies between his earlier and later doctrines or whether he was aware of these inconsistencies but was unable to formulate completely a new and more adequate theory.

The most promising of his late additions to his theory is his distinction, towards the end of the first volume of the *System,* between "material" and "formal" goodness. The distinction is as follows:

An action is *materially* good when in fact it tends to the interest of the system, so far as we can judge of its tendency, or to the good of some part consistent with that of the system, whatever were the affections of the agent. An action is *formally* good when it flowed from good affection in a just proportion.[7]

In making this distinction Hutcheson moves towards the position of Mill's *Utilitarianism* in which Mill makes a similar distinction between motive and intention.[8] And "material goodness" is described by Hutcheson in a sentence which had been used as early as in the *Inquiry,* namely, ". . . that action is best, which procures the greatest happiness for the greatest numbers; and that, worst, which, in like manner, occasions misery."[9] Had Hutcheson presented earlier this distinction between "material" and "formal goodness," his theory would have been much improved and, had he developed it further, it is possible that he might have avoided some of the difficulties which we encountered in his theory of the moral sense and its relationship to motivation.

---

[7] Hutcheson, *System,* I, 252.
[8] John Stuart, Mill, *Utilitarianism* in *John Stuart Mill: Utilitarianism, Liberty, and Representative Government* (London: J. M. Dent & Sons Ltd., 1947), p. 17.
[9] Selby-Bigge, *British Moralists,* I, 107.

CHAPTER V

CONCLUDING REMARKS

The avowed purpose of this book has been to examine Hutcheson's theory
of motivation and of the moral sense and to show that, when combined,
they lead to philosophical perplexities. I have maintained, also, that
philosophical perplexity here, as in most cases, is not the result of mistakes
in fact, but of mistaken efforts to include certain data within a conceptual
framework into which they will not fit. No doubt my attempt to draw
attention to and describe the causes of certain philosophical perplexities
in Hutcheson entails no obligation to suggest how these might be re-
placed by an adequate theory. This, after all, would require a study of
extraordinary scope. I should like, however, to present some concluding
remarks. These will serve as a summary of some of the specific suggestions
growing out of the issues discussed in this book and concerning ways in
which the difficulties inherent in Hutcheson's theory might be avoided.
My concluding remarks will be closely interrelated and will be directed
to the following topics: (1) the moral sense and moral feelings; (2) the
justification of moral judgments; (3) the nature of moral judgments;
(4) motivation and the moral sense.

THE MORAL SENSE AND MORAL FEELINGS

One of Hutcheson's main concerns in the *Inquiry* is to draw attention
to certain pleasures and pains which can not be traced to self-love. Among
these are approval and disapproval. As a moral philosopher, he believes
that one of his tasks is to call attention to certain of these irreducible data
of perception which others, notably the egoists, had neglected or tried to
reduce to self-love. In this task which he sets himself he shows ability and
accuracy in charting introspective maps.

It is the task itself which needs to be called into question. Although the
search for introspective data may not be without interest, it fails to

provide the sort of explanations of moral judgments and conduct which we require. According to Hutcheson's introspective method, a feeling of approval is certainly more open to inspection than the beliefs upon which it causally depends. As I argued earlier in detail, there is then no restriction on the extraordinary character of the moral views which might be advocated. Approval, even if that of an impartial spectator, might still be directed towards infanticide, cannibalism, capital punishment, etc.

Instead of the attempt to describe the feeling of approval in terms of certain sensations or data of reflection, it is more profitable, in terms of philosophical method, to appeal to certain explanations which are involved in the very description of the feeling. What emerges as the result of such an appeal is the conviction that approval, as a moral emotion, is not, contrary to Hutcheson, consitutive of whatever moral characteristic is in question. John Rawls, in setting forth the characteristics of moral feelings, includes the claim that "these feelings presuppose the acceptance of certain moral principles which are invoked in their explanation, and in part what distinguish different feelings are the different principles occurring in these explanations; ..." [1] Throughout this book I have maintained that Hutcheson's treatment of moral feelings is open to serious objections and that a more adequate theory would follow some of the directions suggested above.

THE JUSTIFICATION OF MORAL JUDGMENTS

There is no need to repeat earlier material attesting to the worth of Hutcheson's distinction between "exciting" and "justifying" reasons and of his discussion in general of justification in morals. It is important, however, to recall the conclusions we arrived at concerning the rather extraordinary position concerning moral justification which, upon close inspection, Hutcheson was found to hold. His view appears to be that the approval of the moral sense is itself the source of all justification by reasons. Ardal suggests that such a view may be ascribed to Hume. Ardal says of Hume:

Perhaps what he means to convey is simply this: when we have a certain peculiar sort of feeling, which we call a feeling of blame, on contemplating a certain action or individual's character, no more need be present in the situation in order that we may be justified in pronouncing the act or character vicious.[2]

[1] John Rawls, "The Sense of Justice," *The Philosophical Review,* LXXII, No. 3 (1963), 298.
[2] Ardal, *Passion and Value,* p. 203.

In a review of Ardal's book, Flew complains that "unfortunately, Ardal does not ask what sort of justification this is supposed to be." [3] Since Hume's position is in these respects very similar to that of Hutcheson, a similar complaint may be directed towards the latter's theory. It may be objected, therefore, that if approval and disapproval are the sorts of introspectible feelings which Hutcheson says they are, then what we commonly mean by justification in morals is certainly neither the expression of such feelings nor the statement that one has them. Why then should Hutcheson have fallen into the error of misdescribing justification in this fashion? This may be attributed, like some of his other errors, to his failure to recognize that approval is a moral feeling which is tied to certain explanations in terms of moral principles. Justifying reasons involve appeals to such principles, not to an introspectible feeling.

The view which Frankena ascribes mistakenly to Hutcheson is therefore a view which the latter might have done well to have adopted. According to this view, moral judgments are based on reasons in the sense that there are justifying reasons which do not presuppose the approval of the moral sense. And, compared to the view Hutcheson actually holds, this is surely a more acceptable account of justifying reasons and their relationship to approval and the moral sense.

There is one part of Hutcheson's account of justification which calls for a final comment, namely, his treatment or benevolence as a justifying reason. Hutcheson maintains that the cause of moral approval is our viewing of acts performed from benevolent motives. Approval is here causally tied to a natural motive. And, it might be added, Hutcheson does not include among such natural motives desires to act justly, to tell the truth, and to do our duty. Hence, such natural motives being absent, benevolence becomes the more attractive as the single candidate for the cause of approval.

We have already discussed the difficulties arising from this account of benevolence as a justifying reason. In framing a more adequate theory, it is of interest to ask to what extent these difficulties would have been avoided if Hutcheson had held the position ascribed to him by Frankena. Here it must be concluded that although the theory which Frankena ascribes to Hutcheson is in many respects more attractive than that which the latter actually holds, the theory ascribed to him by Frankena is open to a serious objection concerning the issue in question, namely, the treatment of benevolence as a justifying reason. Frankena ascribes to Hutche-

---

[3] Antony Flew, review of *Passion and Value in Hume's Treatise*, by Pall S. Ardal, in *The Journal of Philosophy*, LXV, No. 9 (1968), 260.

son the view that "there is ultimately only one justifying reason, namely, benevolent intention or tendency . . ." [4] But, in framing an adequate theory, it should be objected that it is surely an error to maintain that the single logical ground or justifying reason for approval is benevolent motivation. Indeed, as we conduct a more realistic inquiry into the justifying reasons actually given for moral judgments, we find that we are relieved of the burden of having to tie approval logically to natural attitudes and motives and may even conclude that justifying reasons, especially in the case of moral judgments involving obligatoriness, rightness or wrongness, may not have to do with motives at all. We find, furthermore, that the "beneficence" of an action may constitute a justifying reason, meaning by a "beneficent action," not an action having a certain motive, but an action which does good to others. And, having found a place for "beneficence," we need not suppose that either "beneficence" or "benevolence" need be selected as the single ultimate justifying reason. Hutcheson's emphasis on benevolence is commendable; his exclusion of all other justifying reasons is simply an error. Among the justifying reasons which may be given for moral judgments we may surely include that the act in question involves the keeping of a promise, that it is just, that it is deserved, that it leads to the best possible consequences, and perhaps even other considerations.

THE NATURE OF MORAL JUDGMENTS

It might be best to begin with a brief summary of the conclusions arrived at in Chapter II concerning Hutcheson's theory as it relates to the topic of moral judgments. In Chapter II I concluded that Hutcheson could best be described as holding one of two positions, the one, a form of the Subjective Theory, the other, a form of non-cognitivism. The form of the Subjective Theory to which his view is most closely related is a type of naturalism according to which moral judgments refer to the unique feeling of pleasure or approval which would be felt by an ideal observer. The form of non-cognitivism best ascribed to Hutcheson is that according to which moral judgments are expressive of approval and at the same time include certain claims about this approval, claims to the effect that this approval is that which would be experienced by an "ideal spectator."

Is one of the above interpretations of Hutcheson's theory to be preferred? I argued that Frankena overstates the case for a non-cognitivist interpretation. However, I maintained that there is a slight presumption

[4] Frankena, "Hutcheson's Moral Sense Theory," p. 375.

that Hutcheson would favor a non-cognitive theory. This presumption rests mainly on the fact that Hutcheson does not seem to be proposing the sort of statistical investigation of actual or possible feelings of approval which is required by the trans-subjective form of the Subjective Theory. Quite apart from Hutcheson's own intentions and preferences, I suggested that in view of the familiar charges that would be brought against a naturalistic interpretation of Hutcheson, it is of considerable interest to examine the possibility of a non-cognitivist interpretation.

But at the end of Chapter II I claimed that the non-cognitive view which I had ascribed to Hutcheson was open to fatal objections which ran parallel to those which Broad levelled at the trans-subjective, dispositional form of the Subjective Theory. Broad's objections are condensed into three questions:

(1) Can it deal with the fact that judgments like "That act is right" seem always to be grounded upon the presence in the act of some non-ethical right-inclining characteristic, such as being the fulfilment of a promise? (ii) If so, can it deal with the further fact that the connection between a right-inclining characteristic and the rightness which it tends to convey seems to be necessary and synthetic? And (iii) can it deal with the fact that it seems not only intelligible but also true to say that the moral pro-emotion is felt towards an act in respect of the characteristic of *rightness* and moral anti-emotion in respect of the characteristic of *wrongness?* [5]

In making moral judgments expressive of approval and, at the same time, presenting an introspectionist account of approval, Hutcheson sunders approval from its logical connection with acts and character-dispositions. Thus he is at a loss to account for those characteristics of moral discourse and moral reasoning reflected in Broad's objections. For Hutcheson, it can only be contingent that moral judgments are grounded upon the presence of benevolence. Furthermore, since, according to Hutcheson, approval is constitutive of the moral characteristic, he can allow no sense in which approval is felt as a result of the presence of some characteristic of rightness attaching to an act.

In order to clarify certain characteristics of Hutcheson's actual position and to show some of the alternatives to his theory, I propose to examine briefly a position outlined by George Kerner. I should like to insist rather emphatically that my purpose is not to defend Kerner's theory, but to make use of the fact that it has certain logical relationships to the issues under discussion pertaining to Hutcheson's theory.

Kerner, drawing heavily upon ideas contained in the writings of J. L. Austin, presents a study of the linguistic performance "I approve X"

[5] Broad, "Moral-Sense Theories in Ethics," p. 376

which he then proceeds to employ as a model for exploring the nature of moral judgments and moral reasoning. Kerner, following Austin, has occasion to note that ambiguity of the term "approve" to which reference has so often been made. As Austin puts it, " 'I approve' may have the performative force of giving approval or it may have a descriptive meaning: 'I favour this.' " [6] Kerner's analysis concerns the sentence "I approve," rather than the sentence "I approve of." The words "I approve" constitute a linguistic performance not readily assimilated either to descriptions of matters of fact or to what are merely expressions of feelings or attitudes. Kerner claims that "to say 'I approve X' is like saying 'I endorse or certify X is a qualified so-and-so.' " [7] In this respect his position has much in common with that of others such as Toulmin who have on occasion employed what might be called a "gerundival analysis," that is, a type of analysis which consists in the claim, explicit or implicit, that something or other is in some sense "worthy."

It is in his position with respect to the justification of linguistic performances that Kerner owes much to Austin. Kerner contends that moral judgments, and indeed all linguistic performances, involve (1) criteria of application and (2) a characteristic performative force.[8] By "criteria of application" he means that there are certain criteria or rules governing the application of words or expressions. The term "characteristic performative force" refers to the *sort* of speech-act which is being performed. A study of the characteristic performative force of moral judgments would consist of an examination of the relationship of such judgments to expressions of attitudes, decisions, imperatives, and so on. Kerner's view is that the justification of linguistic performances proceeds in two stages which parallel the above distinction between criteria of application and characteristic performative force. The first stage concerns the providing of evidence and the construction of an "evaluative proof" which shows that standards have been met. The second stage goes on to show, in Kerner's terms, that the speaker has certain qualifications which render him competent to make the judgment in question.[9]

The sort of theory which Kerner is here developing has certain attractions. Instead of the vagueness with which some of the non-cognitivist theories refer to the function of moral judgments as expressive, incitive,

[6] J. L. Austin, *How to Do Things with Words* (New York: Oxford University Press, 1965), p. 78.
[7] George C. Kerner, *The Revolution in Ethical Theory* (Oxford: Oxford University Press, 1966), p. 212.
[8] *Ibid.*, p. 25.
[9] *Ibid.*, p. 212.

etc., Kerner, following Austin, proposes an exhaustive and painstaking study of the characteristic performative force of moral judgments. In addition, Austin's models suggest new ways of looking at justification and moral reasoning. But further elaboration and critical evaluation of this type of theory is beyond the scope of my investigation and I shall restrict myself to a few observations relevant to the issues under discussion as related to Hutcheson.

It would be utterly fanciful to suppose that Hutcheson subscribes to the sort of Austinian theory we have been considering. However, a few comparisons may be illuminating and point to directions which an adequate ethical theory might take. Let us consider first that stage of justification which, according to Kerner, has to do with the competence, sincerity, and other needed qualifications of the person who performs the speech-act in question. Many of these qualifications have their parallels in the theory which I have ascribed to Hutcheson. These are the kinds of qualifications which Hutcheson would connote by the term "ideal spectator." And, as Hutcheson indicates, this "ideal spectator" is identified with what I myself approve upon reflection. According to the theory which I ascribed to Hutcheson, moral judgments are expressive of approval and, at the same time, include claims to the effect that the approval expressed is that of the ideal spectator. These claims express requirements of moral discourse and, as I argued earlier, these requirements that the approval be that of an ideal spectator are logical and not merely causal requirements. These requirements, therefore, may be seen to fulfil in part the sort of conditions referred to by Kerner as having to do with the competence, sincerity, and other needed qualifications of the person who performs the speech-act in question.

Let us turn next to the other stage of justification discussed by Kerner, namely, the stage which has to do with "criteria of application" and the elaboration of proofs in terms of standards. It is in this area that Hutcheson's theory is deficient. If my interpretation is correct, justification for Hutcheson ends with a deliverance of the moral sense in the form of the reaction of approval or disapproval, always qualifying this by adding that the approval in question is that of an "ideal spectator." As I have noted before, this approval, even when qualified in this fashion, is still lacking in those logical connections with its objects which seem to be reflected in our language. The result is that since approval might be directed towards all sorts of objects, e.g. genocide, glue-sniffing, cannibalism, etc., there is no limit to the "weird moral views," as Philippa Foot calls them, which might be held. Hutcheson is in error in supposing or suggesting that approval is an immediately introspectible feeling which can be adequately described without involving an explanation of the conditions under which we have this feeling. From Kerner's point of view, therefore, Hutcheson's theory would be found deficient in its failure to do justice to that stage of justification which has to do with "criteria of application" and the elaboration of proofs in terms of standards.

It is of interest to note that the theory which Frankena ascribes to Hutcheson would avoid some of the above deficiencies relating to that type of justification having to do with the elaboration of proofs in terms of standards. However I have argued at length that this theory cannot be attributed to Hutcheson. According to Frankena's interpretation, justifying reasons can be given for the emotional reaction of the moral sense, thus avoiding the objections raised against cutting off approval from its logical conditions.

Thus, on the one hand, the theory which I ascribed to Hutcheson fulfils many of the requirements for that stage of justification described by Kerner and having to do with the competence, sincerity and other needed qualifications of the person who performs the speech-act in question. On the other hand, the theory ascribed to Hutcheson by Frankena fulfils at least some of the requirements for the other stage of justification described by Kerner, the stage having to do with criteria of application and the elaboration of proofs. If, therefore, the theories ascribed to Hutcheson by Frankena and myself were to be combined, an attractive theory would result. Although it would not fulfil all of the detailed conditions envisaged by Austinian studies of the characteristic performance force of speech-acts, it would be able to account for the two levels of justification, the one in terms of standards or criteria for approval, the other in terms of the ideal qualifications of the person who issues the moral judgment. Furthermore, this theory would be able to meet Broad's formidable objections, quoted earlier, to the trans-subjective, dispositional form of the Subjective Theory. In maintaining that approval is logically tied to certain acts and character-dispositions, it may now be held with Broad that the relationship between benevolence and moral characteristics is not merely contingent. One might, however, like some of the exponents of the "good reasons" approach, attempt to defend a conception of moral reasoning which, although holding to a logical relationship between Broad's "right-inclining characteristics" and rightness, shuns his appeal to synthetic a priori truths.

Serious criticism would still be forthcoming from two directions. First, criticism might still be directed towards the sorts of reasons for moral judgments described by Frankena in his interpretation of Hutcheson. Ultimately, on his interpretation, there is only one justifying reason, namely, benevolence. Critics, beginning with Butler, have insisted that not all justifying reasons can be comprehended under this single term. Are there not, they ask, reasons which appeal to distributive justice, promise-keeping, truth-telling, and so on, and which are not subsumable under benevolence? Secondly, as discussed earlier, it might be objected that moral approval may be directed not only to motives and character-dispositions but to acts as such. Critics who take this line of attack have sometimes accused Hutcheson and Hume of having developed theories of moral goodness and virtue, but not of moral obligation. The difficulties which Hutcheson encounters in developing his theory of obligation and motivation lend support to this charge.

MOTIVATION AND THE MORAL SENSE

In his conception of a moral sense which is a source both of justification and of excitement, Hutcheson hoped to provide an answer to all of the questions which might be raised concerning the relationship between "is" and "ought" and between motivation and obligation. Much of this book has been devoted to pointing out the difficulties which result when Hutcheson's theory of motivation is combined with his moral sense doctrine.

Let us recall, in brief summary, some of these difficulties. Hutcheson seems forced by his own assumptions into either or both of two untenable views. According to the first, what we ought to do is to act from benevolent motives. According to the second, our motive in doing as we ought is a desire to act from an approved motive. On both of these views, Hutcheson must be considered an externalist as regards the relationship between moral judgments and motivation. That is, the desire which follows that approval of the moral sense which is expressed by moral judgments is contingent, not necessary. The internalist may nevertheless remark upon the extreme closeness of the connection between obligation and motivation in Hutcheson, a closeness which leads the internalist to question whether or not the "desire for moral excellence" and the desire to do as one ought are as empirically grounded as Hutcheson would have us believe.

I shall not attempt to set forth an adequate and complete account of how obligation and motivation should be treated, an account which is beyond the scope of this book. However, I should like to reflect briefly on how a theory of the sort proposed by Hutcheson might be amended or corrected as regards the problem of the relationship between obligation and motivation.

In the preceding section of this chapter I made suggestions concerning a theory of the nature and function of moral judgments, especially as such a theory relates to the employment of the term "approval." Following Kerner, I contended that the justification of moral judgments involves (1) criteria of application and (2) a characteristic performative force. I argued, furthermore, that, considered in this light, Hutcheson's theory is lacking as regards the first of these, fairly close to the requirements of the second. That is, Hutcheson, if interpreted rather freely, might be said to include most of those features having to do with the competence, sincerity, and ideal qualifications of the person who makes a moral judgment. However, Hutcheson's treatment of approval as lacking any logical ties with its objects is such as to render him subject to the criticism of having failed to include the appeal to "criteria of application."

What, then, if Hutcheson were to have included both of the above sorts of justification, namely, those referred to as involving criteria of application and a characteristic performative force? What would be the relationship between such justification and motivation?

To begin with, the adoption of such an account of justification would mean that justification is not grounded, as Hutcheson actually held, in reasons which head up in the approval of the moral sense. Instead, justification includes reasons which maintain that something or other is worthy of approval. Furthermore, it need not be supposed that such justifying reasons can only motivate, as Hutcheson believed, through the fact that the approval of the moral sense generates desire. Surely, it might be argued, such justifying reasons are themselves motivational.

But the contention that justifying reasons are themselves motivational requires closer examination. According to some extreme internalist, it might be held that having a justifying reason logically entails having motivation. This is the sort of view of the relationship between moral judgments and motivation which was held by Richard Price when he stated that "when we are conscious that an action is fit to be done, or that it *ought* to be done, it is not conceivable that we can remain uninfluenced, or want a *motive* to action." [10] It is against this type of view that Broad objects as follows:

[10] Price, *Review*, p. 186.

So far as I can see, there would not be the slightest inconsistency in supposing that a being who was rational in the ethically neutral sense, and did in fact have the ideas of right and wrong and make moral judgments, was completely devoid of specifically moral emotion and conation.[11]

It is simply not self-contradictory for a person both to maintain that a certain action is right and that he has no motive for performing it.

What meaning shall then be given to the claim under investigation that justifying reasons are themselves motivational? The externalist will claim that justifying reasons may simply evoke pro-attitudes in some, many, or most human beings. Such pro-attitudes are contingent, nor necessary. One may know the right or may know justifying reasons for actions and yet fail to be motivated. This position is subject to the charge that it fails to appreciate the closeness of the connection between moral judgments, justifying reasons, and motivation.

How then shall we avoid the dilemma of an internalism which insists on an entailment between justifying reasons and motives and an externalism which fails to appreciate the closeness of the connection between justifying reasons and motivations?

In tracing only a few of the directions which an adequate reply to this question might take, I should begin by drawing attention to what some writers such as Nowell-Smith and Philippa Foot have sometimes referred to as the "action guiding" function of moral and practical discourse. To give a justifying reason, in Hutcheson's sense, or to declare an action to be right, need not be to designate some property, whether natural or non-natural, but may be, among other things, to guide and direct action.

The obvious retort is to point out that moral judgments can guide action only if there are antecedent wants or desires and that, in Hutcheson's terms, justifying reasons can excite to action only if they involve passions or affections. At this point let us recall Nowell-Smith's use of the term "contextual implication":

I shall say that a statement *p* contextually implies a statement *q* if anyone who knew the normal conventions of the language would be entitled to infer *q* from *p* *in the context in which they occur*.[12]

We may now go on to maintain, following Nowell-Smith, that no moral judgment is action-guiding in the sense that motivation is logically entailed and such that it would be logically self-contradictory to maintain both "I ought to do X" and "I have no motive whatsoever for perform-

[11] Broad, "Moral-Sense Theories in Ethics," p. 384.
[12] Nowell-Smith, *Ethics,* p. 80.

ing X." Nevertheless, it is not merely a contingent fact that we want to do what we ought to do. Although being obliged and wanting to do as we ought are logically distinct, these are among those sorts of things which, according to Nowell-Smith, "normally go along together" and which are therefore such that "the 'contingent' connections between them become enshrined in the logic of the language." [13]

It may not be too farfetched to suggest that the appeal which the moral sense theorists made to the constitution of the universe and to the constitution of human nature reflected their concern to assure a close connection between moral judgments and human motivation. But, as discussed earlier, this, like most appeals to an ideal human nature, suffers from the intolerable vagueness and ambiguity of the term "natural" which they employed sometimes as descriptive, sometimes as normative, and which was attended with the appeal to final causes.

Returning to the sort of position advanced by Nowell-Smith, it seems to me that on his theory the relationship between moral discourse and motivation is in danger of being conceived of as closer than it actually is. I should want to maintain that, generally speaking, moral discourse is action-guiding and "contextually implies" the presence of motivation. However, even granting the limitations of context, it seems incredible to suppose that no gap can ever exist between a judgment such as "I ought to do X" and my motivation. To suppose that, in context, no such gap occurs is to suppose the existence of what I have called "instant motivation" as concomitant with any such moral judgment. On such a view, no person who took a more enlightened view of his obligations could fail to match his views with enlightened motivation. Even if we grant that, generally speaking, moral judgments are practical, action-guiding, and involve some logical or quasi-logical connection with wanting, it seems implausible to suppose that there might not be particular cases in which an agent might make a moral judgment and yet suffer some "gap" or "lag" between this judgment and motivation. Where such gaps exist, it is not the function of the moral philosopher to remove them, nor indeed to bemoan their existence.

In this concluding chapter I have been making some comments pertaining to issues growing out of Hutcheson's theory. Further comments would, I suspect, require the sort of full-scale investigation of moral discourse and its relationship to motivation which cannot here be undertaken.

[13] *Ibid.*, p. 99.

SELECTED BIBLIOGRAPHY

BOOKS

Aaron, Richard I. *John Locke*. 2d ed. Oxford: Clarendon Press, 1955.
Aiken, Henry D., ed. *Hume's Moral and Political Philosophy*. New York: Hafner Publishing Company, 1948.
Albee, Ernest. *A History of English Utilitarianism*. London: George Allen and Unwin Ltd., 1901.
Anscombe, G. E. M. *Intention*. Oxford: Basil Blackwell, 1958.
Ardal, Pall S. *Passion and Value in Hume's Treatise*. Edinburgh: Edinburgh University Press, 1966.
Aristotle *Nicomachean Ethics*. Translated by W. D. Ross. *The Basic Works of Aristotle*. Edited by Richard McKeon. New York: Random House, 1941.
Austin, J. L. *How To Do Things with Words*. New York: Oxford University Press, 1965.
Blackstone, William T. *Francis Hutcheson and Contemporary Ethical Theory*. Athens: University of Georgia Press, 1965.
Bonar, James. *Moral Sense*. New York: Macmillan Company, 1930.
Boswell, James. *Boswell's Life of Johnson*. Edited by George B. Hill. 6 vols. Oxford: Clarendon Press, 1934-50.
Brandt, Richard B. *Ethical Theory*. Englewood Cliffs, N.J.: Prentice-Hall, Inc., 1959.
Broad, C. D. *Ethics and the History of Philosophy*. New York: Humanities Press, Inc., 1952.
—. *Five Types of Ethical Theory*. London: Routledge and Kegan Paul Ltd., 1930.
Broiles, R. David. *The Moral Philosophy of David Hume*. The Hague: Martinus Nijhoff, 1964.
Chappell, V. C., ed. *Modern Studies in Philosophy: Hume*. Anchor Books. Garden City, New York: Doubleday & Company, Inc., 1966.
Cooper, Anthony Ashley, Third Earl of Shaftesbury. *Characteristics of Men, Manners, Opinions, Times*. Edited by John H. Robinson. 2 vols. New York: Bobbs-Merrill Company, Inc., 1964.
Dewey, John, and Tufts, James H. *Ethics*. rev. ed. New York: Henry Holt and Company, 1936.
Fowler, Thomas. *Shaftesbury and Hutcheson*. New York: G. P. Putnam's Sons, 1883.

Frankena, William K. *Ethics.* Foundations of Philosophy Series. Edited by Elizabeth and Monroe Beardsley. Englewood Cliffs, N.J.: Prentice-Hall, Inc., 1963.

Gibson, James. *Locke's Theory of Knowledge and its Historical Relations.* Cambridge, Eng.: Cambridge University Press, 1960.

Greig, J. Y. T., ed. *The Letters of David Hume.* 2 vols. Oxford: Clarendon Press, 1932.

Hume, David. *Enquiries Concerning the Human Understanding and Concerning the Principles of Morals.* 2d ed. Oxford: Clarendon Press, 1902.

—. *A Treatise of Human Nature.* Edited by L. A. Selby-Bigge. Oxford: Clarendon Press, 1958.

Hutcheson, Francis. *An Essay on the Nature and Conduct of the Passions, with Illustrations upon the Moral Sense.* 4th ed. London: Printed for W. Innys et al., 1756.

—. *An Inquiry into the Original of our Ideas of Beauty and Virtue, In Two Treatises I. Inquiry Concerning Beauty, Order, Harmony and Design, and II. Inquiry Concerning Moral Good and Evil.* 5th ed. London: R. Ware, 1753.

—. *Reflections Upon Laughter, and Remarks upon the Fable of the Bees.* Glasgow: Printed by R. Urie for D. Baxter, 1750.

—. *A Short Introduction to Moral Philosophy in three books containing the Elements of Ethics and the Law of Nature.* Translated from the Latin. Glasgow: R. Foulis, 1747.

—. *A System of Moral Philosophy.* 2 vols. London: A. Millar, 1755.

Kant, Immanuel. *Foundations of the Metaphysics of Morals. Immanuel Kant: Critique of Practical Reason and Other Writings in Moral Philosophy.* Translated and edited by Lewis White Beck. Chicago: University of Chicago Press, 1949.

Kemp, J. *Reason, Action and Morality.* London: Routledge and Kegan Paul, 1964.

Kerner, George C. *The Revolution in Ethical Theory.* Oxford: Oxford University Press, 1966.

Kydd, Rachael M. *Reason and Conduct in Hume's Treatise.* New York: Russell & Russell Inc., 1964.

Ladd, John. *The Structure of a Moral Code.* Cambridge, Mass.: Harvard University Press, 1957.

Locke, John. *An Essay Concerning Human Understanding.* 2 vols. London: J. M. Dent & Sons Ltd., 1961.

Malebranche, Nicholas. *Treatise Concerning the Search after Truth.* Translated by T. Taylor. London: L. Lichfield, 1674.

Mandeville, Bernard. *The Fable of the Bees.* Edited by F. B. Kaye. 2 vols. Oxford: Clarendon Press, 1924.

Martineau, James. *Types of Ethical Theory.* 2 vols., 3d ed. rev. Oxford: Clarendon Press, 1891.

Mayo, Bernard. *Ethics and the Moral Life.* London: Macmillan & Co. Ltd., 1958.

Melden, A. I. *Free Action.* London: Routledge & Kegan Paul, 1961.

Mill, John Stuart. *Utilitarianism. John Stuart Mill: Utilitarianism, Liberty,*

and Representative Government. London: J. M. Dent & Sons Ltd., 1947.
Moore, George Edward. *Principia Ethica*. Cambridge, Eng.: Cambridge University Press, 1948.
Morley, Henry, ed. *The Spectator*. 3 vols. London: George Rutledge and Sons, Limited, 1891.
Nowell-Smith, P. H. *Ethics*. London: Penguin Books, Ltd., 1954.
Perry, Ralph Barton. *Realms of Value*. Cambridge, Mass.: Harvard University Press, 1954.
Peters, R. S. *The Concept of Motivation*. London: Routledge & Kegan Paul, 1958.
Plato *The Republic*. *The Dialogues of Plato*. Translated by B. Jowett. 2 vols. New York: Random House, 1937.
Price, Richard. *A Review of the Principal Questions in Morals*. Edited by D. Daiches Raphael. Oxford: Clarendon Press, 1948.
Prichard, H. A. *Moral Obligation*. Oxford: Clarendon Press, 1949.
Prior, Arthur N. *Logic and the Basis of Ethics*. Oxford: Clarendon Press, 1949.
Rand, Benjamin, ed. *The Life, Unpublished Letters, and Philosophical Regimen of Anthony, Earl of Shaftesbury*. London: Swann Sonnenschien & Co., Ltd., 1900.
Raphael, D. Daiches. *The Moral Sense*. London: Oxford University Press, 1947.
Rogers, A. K. *Morals in Review*. New York: Macmillan Company, 1927.
Ross, Sir W. David. *Foundations of Ethics*. Oxford: Clarendon Press, 1939.
Ryle, Gilbert. *The Concept of Mind*. New York: Barnes & Noble, Inc., 1949.
Scott, William Robert. *Francis Hutcheson*. Cambridge, Eng.: Cambridge University Press, 1900.
Selby-Bigge, L. A., ed. *British Moralists*. 2 vols. Indianapolis: Bobbs Merrill Company, Inc., 1964.
Sharp, Frank Chapman. *Ethics*. New York: Century Co., 1928.
Sidgwick, Henry. *The Methods of Ethics*. 2d ed. London: Macmillan and Co., 1877.
—. *Outlines of the History of Ethics*. London: Macmillan and Co., Limited, 1949.
Smith, Norman Kemp. *The Philosophy of David Hume*. London: Macmillan and Co., Limited, 1949.
Stephen, Sir Leslie. *History of English Thought in the Eighteenth Century*. 2 vols. New York: G. P. Putnam's Sons, 1902.
Stevenson, Charles L. *Ethics and Language*. New Haven: Yale University Press, 1944.
Walsh, James Jerome. *Aristotle's Conception of Moral Weakness*. New York: Columbia University Press, 1963.
Wolfson, Harry Austryn. *The Philosophy of Spinoza*. 2 vols. New York: Meridian Books, Inc., 1958.

ESSAYS AND ARTICLES

Anscombe, G. E. M. "Thought and Action in Aristotle." *New Essays on Plato and Aristotle.* Edited by Renford Bambrough. London: Routledge and Kegan Paul, 1965.

Broad, C. D. "Some Reflections on Moral-Sense Theories in Ethics." *Readings in Ethical Theory.* Edited by Herbert Feigl and John Hospers. New York: Appleton-Century-Crofts, Inc., 1952.

Falk, W. D. " 'Ought' and Motivation." *Readings in Ethical Theory.* Edited ben Wilfrid Sellars and John Hospers. New York: Appleton-Century-Crofts, Inc., 1952.

Flew, Anthony. Review of *Passion and Value in Hume's Treatise,* by Pall S. Ardal. *The Journal of Philosophy,* LXV, No. 9 (1968), 257-60.

Foot, Philippa. "Hume on Moral Judgment." *David Hume: A Symposium.* Edited by D. F. Pears. London: Macmillan & Co. Ltd., 1963.

Frankena, William K. "Hutcheson's Moral Sense Theory." *Journal of the History of Ideas,* XVI, No. 3 (1955), 356-75.

—. "Obligation and Motivation in Recent Philosophy." *Essays in Moral Philosophy.* Edited by A. I. Melden. Seattle: University of Washington Press, 1958.

Green, Thomas Hill. "Introduction to the Moral Part of Hume's Treatise." *Works of Thomas Hill Green.* Edited by R. L. Nettleship. Vol. I. London: Longmans, Green and Co., 1906.

Ladd, John. "The Desire to Do One's Duty for Its Own Sake." *Morality and the Language of Conduct.* Edited by Hector-Neri Castaneda and George Nakhnikian. Detroit: Wayne State University Press, 1963.

McGilvary, E. E. "Altruism in Hume's Treatise." *The Philosophical Review,* XII, No. 3 (1903), 275-95.

Peach, Bernard. "Francis Hutcheson and the Problem of Justification." Unpublished paper read at the Joint Philosophy Colloquium between Duke University and the University of North Carolina, December, 1956.

Rawls, John. "The Sense of Justice." *The Philosophical Review,* LXXII, No. 3 (1963), 282-93.

Smith, James Ward. "The British Moralists and the Fallacy of Psychologism." *Journal of the History of Ideas,* XI, No. 2 (1950), 159-78.

Stevenson, Charles L. "The Emotive Meaning of Ethical Terms." *Readings in Ethical Theory.* Edited by Wilfrid Sellars and John Hospers. New York: Appleton-Century-Crofts, Inc., 1952.

Sypher, Wylie. "Hutcheson and the 'Classical' Theory of Slavery." *Journal of Negro History,* XXIV, No. 3 (1939), 263-80.

INDEX

Aaron, Richard I., 44-45
"action-guiding" function of practical
  discourse, 120-121
Addison, Joseph, 42
affections, 10-12, 23-24
Aiken, Henry D., 93
Allan, D. J., 27
Anscombe, G. E. M., 27, 88, 105
approval
  and moral judgments, 51 ff.
  as a kind of pleasure, 43
  as a simple idea, 43
Ardal, Pall S., 49, 62, 111
"argument from trivialization," 100
Aurelius, Marcus, 5
Austin, J. L., 114-117

Balguy, John, 100
beneficence, 85, 92, 113
benevolence, 13, 83-88, 91-95, 112-113,
  117-118
Blackstone, William T., 59
Boswell, James, 19
Brandt, Richard, 63
Broad, C. D., 14, 44, 49-51, 64-65, 77,
  84, 99, 114, 119
Burnet, Gilbert, 3, 72
Butler, Joseph, 1, 3, 4, 8, 23, 36, 46, 84,
  90, 97, 107

calm desires, 13, 23 ff., 76
"characteristic performative force," 115,
  119
Cicero, 5, 36
Clarke, Samuel, 1-2, 4, 26, 68, 70-74,
  77-79, 89, 99, 103
conformity to reason, 72, 75
conformity to truth, 72-75, 78
conscience, 106-108

and authority, 97, 107-108
constitution, nature as a, 46
contextual implication, 120-121
criteria of application, 116-117, 119
Cudworth, Ralph, 1, 3, 14
Cumberland, Richard, 14, 36

Descartes, R., 36
desire
  a simple idea, 23
  and uneasiness, 11
  as pure affection, 24
  calm, 13, 23 ff., 76
  passionate, 24
Dewey, John, quoted, 84
distributive justice, 118
"double-desire paradox,' 94
"double-version theory," 27-30
duty, sense of, 92 ff.

egoism
  ethical, 15, 68
  psychological, 14-19
empiricism, 39
exciting reasons, 75, 80-83
externalism 66-67, 79, 98-99, 102-105,
  118-120

Falk, W. D., 66
final causes, 46
fittingness, 69, 71-72, 77
Flew, Antony, 112
Foot, Philippa, 60, 103-104, 120
Frankena, William K., 32, 46-47, 55-56,
  64-66, 80-82, 102, 105, 112-113

Gibson, James, 44
good
  formally, 109

materially, 109
natural, 40
"good reasons" position, 59
greatest happiness of the greatest number, 2, 109
Green, T. H., 22, 95

Hampshire, S., 32, 88, 105
hedonic calculus, 2
hedonism, psychological, 14-22
Hobbes, Thomas, 3, 13, 14, 35
Hubermann, Bronislaw, 94
Hume, David, 1-4, 18-19, 46, 51, 59, 62, 68, 74, 76, 82, 84, 86, 90, 92-93, 95, 101-104, 107-108
"Hume's gap,' 103-104

ideal naturalism, 53-54
ideal spectator, 53-65, 113, 116
ideas
    of reflection, 41
    of sensation, 40-41
    simple, 32, 39, 43
"instant motivation," 104, 121
internal sense, 41, 44
internalism, 66-68, 98-99, 102-103
intuitionism, 71 ff.

justifying reasons, 55-59, 75, 80-83, 119-120

Kant, Immanuel, 90
Kerner, George, 114-119
Kydd, Rachael M., 28-29, 67, 81-82, 89, 101-102

Ladd, John, 93n., 97, 99
Leechman, William, 5
Locke, John, 1, 9, 11, 15, 24, 36, 41, 43, 56, 78

Malebranche, N., 8, 36
Mandeville, B., 1, 14, 35
Martineau, James, 48, 85
Mayo, Bernard, 97
McGilvary, E. B., 21
Melden, A. I., 33
Mill, John Stuart, 109
Moore, G. E., 21, 60, 77
moral sense
    and authority, 107-109
    defined, 43
    faculty of perceiving moral

excellence, 107
moral sense theory
    naively realistic form of, 44, 49
    non-cognitive forms of, 50. 57-58, 113-115
    subjective form of, 50-53, 113-114
More, Henry, 14, 43

naturalism, 51 ff.
    ideal, 53-54
Nowell-Smith, P. H., 16, 19, 30-31, 66, 84-85, 88, 92, 96-97, 120-121

obligation
    "interested," 90, 98
    moral, 49, 69, 81, 89-91,94 ff.

passion, 10, 32
Peach, Bernard, 59
Perry, Ralph Barton, 22
Peters, R. S., 33
phenomenalist versus causal analysis, 51
Plato, 8, 13, 23, 26, 36
pleasure
    and natural good, 40
    as a sensation, 40
    as cause of desire, 21-22
    as object of desire, 21-22
Price, Richard, 74, 77, 80, 119
Prichard, H. A., 66, 80, 92, 101
Prior, Arthur N., 82, 100, 102
psychological egoism, 14-19
psychological hedonism, 14-22

qualities
    primary, 41
    secondary, 40

Raphael, D. Daiches, 77, 85, 108
rationalism, 1, 68 ff., 70
Rawls, John, 111
reason
    and ends, 27
    as a motive to action, 25 ff.
    as "oblique ' cause of action, 28
    for doing, 44
reasonableness of actions, 69, 70-71, 76
reasons
    exciting, 75, 80-83
    justifying, 55-59, 75, 80-83, 119-120
representationalism, 44
Ross, W. D., 79
Ryle, Gilbert, 25, 32, 88, 105

self-contradiction in action, 71
self-love, 13, 25, 84-86
sense
  defined, 40
  internal, 41, 44
  reflex, 38, 41-42
Shaftesbury, 1, 3, 9, 35-40, 42, 46-48,
  67-68, 80
Sharp, F. C., 22
Sidgwick, Henry, 15-16, 70-72, 77, 79-80
slavery, Hutcheson on, 2
Smith, Adam, 4, 18
Smith, James Ward, 46, 48

Smith, Norman Kemp, 10
Socrates, 23
Spinoza, B., 36
Stephen, Leslie, quoted, 9, 73
Stevenson, Charles, L., 57, 66
sympathy, 18
Sypher, Wylie, 2n.

"vanishing moral motive," 96

Walsh, J. J., 27-28, 30
Wolfson, H. A., 10
Wollaston, William, 3, 72-77